Freedom Through Options

The Beginner's Guide to Creating
Wealth and Confidence in Any Market

Stacy Toups

Copyright Page

Freedom Through Options

The Beginner's Guide to Creating Wealth and Confidence in Any Market

© 2025 Stacy Toups

Independently published

First Edition, 2025

ISBN: 979-8-9995713-0-4

For permissions or inquiries, contact:

lakestarllc@yahoo.com

Printed in the United States of America

DISCLAIMER

This book is intended solely for educational and illustrative purposes. The author and Lake Star, LLC (collectively referred to as "The Company") do not provide financial, investment, or trading advice, nor are they licensed or registered with any regulatory authority in any jurisdiction to offer such services.

No representation or warranty is made regarding the accuracy or applicability of the methods described herein to your specific circumstances. The information shared reflects a method of trading currently used by the author and is not a recommendation or guarantee of any particular outcome.

Past performance is not indicative of future results. All charts, graphs, trade examples, and discussions included in this book are for illustrative purposes only and should not be construed as advice or recommendations.

Always do your own research and consult with a qualified, licensed financial advisor before making any trading or investment decisions.

By reading this book, you acknowledge and agree to release The Company, its affiliates, and its successors from any and all liability for damages, losses, or injuries resulting from the use or misuse of the information contained herein.

This book is dedicated to my husband, Todd, who has supported and encouraged me in life. I also dedicate this to my girls, Rachel and Phoebe. May you be able to follow in my footsteps to live a life with financial freedom.

Table of Contents

INTRODUCTION

During the COVID-19 crash of the market, I decided to take a chance and start trading. As with all bear markets, it was only temporary, and the market began to recover. I had hopped in during the dip and did very well. With limited education and knowledge in trading, I did not take the necessary precautions to manage my trades properly. This made my trading profits inconsistent. I wanted more consistency and something I could use to provide financial freedom. I took courses, attended webinars, and read books. Book after book told me stories of people's lives more than educating me about investing and trading. Most were leading me to buy a course. No individual thing gave me everything I needed to trade with consistent profits. I had to learn from many different sources.

Once my profits became consistent, I wanted to teach my daughters how to trade. I wanted to give them the advantage I didn't have. As I began teaching my 16-year-old, I was amazed how quickly she picked up on what I was explaining. When I asked her how she learned that so fast, her reply to me was that I explained it so easily a 4th grader could understand. That set off the light bulb. I decided to put into writing the training for my daughters. This is my way of passing the knowledge through generations and to help others. I wanted to express in this book all the concepts I use to make consistent profits and gain financial freedom.

In no way is this financial advice. It is purely educational. It is written to give anyone with no knowledge of financial instruments the keys to start profiting. By learning these concepts, you will learn to use leverage and keep your risk down. In reading this book, I hope you obtain the education and training needed to be confident and make a difference in your financial well-being.

FINANCIAL FREEDOM

Growing up in the 70s and 80s, I always heard the usual advice: Go to college, get a stable job, and contribute to your 401(k). On the surface, it seemed like solid guidance, but could it actually lead to financial freedom? What if I didn't want to attend college, or even couldn't afford college? Is a college degree required? I decided to go the college route. After graduating from college and starting my career, I diligently invested in my 401(k) and lived below my means, but progress felt slow. Despite devouring books on financial success, including following Warren Buffett's investment strategies, I still hadn't cracked the code to true financial freedom. I was stuck in the rat race. I attended a seminar and bought a book by Robert Kiyosaki titled Rich Dad, Poor Dad. Kiyosaki emphasized having multiple streams of income. Nothing gave me clear instructions on getting the financial freedom I sought. I was always left with more questions, and I just didn't know where to begin. Then, in 2020, the COVID crash hit.

I persuaded my husband to take a stake in individual stocks that had taken a dive. Surprisingly, it paid off, and we made a healthy profit that year. During the COVID lockdown, I came across an investing seminar online. It was usually a weekend class for a few thousand dollars. Because of the COVID lockdown, it was being offered for $500 online.

I gave it a shot. One small segment during this seminar discussed the use of options. So many people I had heard talk about how that's a risky investment. The way I saw it, I could use leverage and have the potential to make much more profits. Could this be what I was looking for to create financial freedom? I had tried what I thought was the Warren Buffett way. I tried the time-consuming fundamental analysis. Who has time for that? Finding undervalued companies in this technology-driven age is practically nonexistent. Everything moves so fast. News is already priced into the stock price. I had been buying a few individual stocks and contributing to my 401k. Every time it looked like the market was doing well, there'd be some bad news, event, or cause for the market to shift direction, and I would spend months trying to make up lost profits. I needed to find a way to financial freedom. What we were doing was not going to get us there before age 65.

There are several stages of what I call "money class." Many people think being rich means the same as being wealthy. There is a difference. Rich are those who make a lot of money and have a lot of money to spend on an extravagant lifestyle. Their status is by their job. Because their job is their means of high income, they could lose their rich status if something were to happen to their job. They cannot maintain the "rich" lifestyle without their career. Being wealthy involves having substantial assets and investments that can provide multiple income streams. The wealthy focus on long-term growth and working towards financial freedom. Financial freedom is the ultimate goal.

Financial freedom is when a person has enough income, assets, or resources to cover their living expenses without relying on a paycheck or working actively for money. It's when someone can choose how they spend their time without the pressure of financial constraints.

Key aspects of financial freedom include:

1. **Passive Income**: Money generated without actively working for it, such as from rental income, royalties, or businesses that run without constant involvement.

2. **Debt Freedom**: Being free from high-interest debt and financial obligations. This often means living within one's means, avoiding consumer debt, and paying off loans like credit cards, student loans, and mortgages.

3. **Emergency Savings**: Having a safety net or an emergency fund large enough to cover months of living expenses in case of unexpected events, such as a job loss,

health crisis, or disaster events like hurricanes, flooding, or fire destruction.

4. **Investments**: Accumulating assets like stocks, bonds, real estate, or businesses that grow in value over time, providing a reliable source of income.

5. **Lifestyle Flexibility**: The ability to choose how and when to work, travel, or pursue hobbies without being dictated by financial needs. It often involves conscious spending and financial planning to align with long-term goals.

Reaching financial freedom is a journey, and it's not just about accumulating wealth—it's about achieving peace of mind, reducing stress, and living life on your terms.

You might be asking, 'How can I obtain financial freedom? Where do I begin?' This book shows you the way with simple strategies for starting to invest and growing your wealth. I will explain how to invest and grow your investments in a way that is so simple that even a fourth grader can understand.

First, let's look at the advice everyone receives about investing in a 401(k). What is a 401(k)? This is your nest egg for retirement. Most people know you can put your money into a savings account and earn interest on the savings. Usually, the interest rate is less than the rate of inflation. Your money loses value sitting in a savings account. You cannot save your way to financial freedom. A 401(k) is a savings plan with investments for growth sponsored by your employer as a benefit for saving and investing for retirement. There are many pros and cons to using a 401(k). Your 401(k) will allow you to make a better return than a savings account. It's a form of passive investing. You contribute with pretax money. If your employer matches a portion of your contributions, those funds are also pretax. The advantage is that you get your employer's company match. If you contribute $1,000 for the year with a company match of 50% of your contributions, that's like getting a 50% return on your money in the first year and having $1,500 in your investments before any gains or losses. But don't let that fool you. That's a one-time return. That remaining $1,500 may not grow as much in the following years. A 401(k) can also lose money. In the 2001 market crash, many people saw years of their 401(k) contributions come crashing down as much as 50%. Imagine having one million dollars in a 401(k), which suddenly drops to 500k. If you were thinking about retiring soon, you now think you'll never get to retire. With a savings account, you don't invest in anything. You earn interest on your money. With your 401(k), you do choose where to invest your money. However, you are limited in which funds you can invest in. You are also restricted from moving money in and out of funds when you expect a swing in the market. When you move out of a fund into another, you must wait several days, usually 30-90, depending on your plan's rules, before moving back into the original fund. For someone who has never had any investment experience, this can be a good start to learn about stocks and funds. Your 401(k) is invested in managed funds. These funds range from index, large-cap, small-cap, foreign, real estate, and bond funds. Some offer a growth or age target fund. You can select what funds to invest in and let them sit. With each paycheck, your employer will handle depositing your contributions into your 401(k) along with their company match. Because the managed funds you invest in are managing the funds for you, they charge a management fee. The fee varies depending on what funds you choose to put your money in. These can range anywhere from 0.5% to 2% of the amount you hold in the fund. For example, if you have $100,000 invested in your 401(k), you might pay between $500 and $2,000 annually in fees, depending on the funds and plan structure. While investing in your 401(k), with exceptions, you cannot take money out until you retire at 55 or turn 59 ½. When you start taking money out of your 401(k), this is referred to as distributions. You pay taxes on your distributions. You are not taxed on the money when you contribute to your 401(k), and it grows tax-free until you take the money out as a distribution. Investing in your 401(k) seems to be excellent advice. But is it? Will this give you financial freedom? Let's look a little closer. Say you go to college and begin an exciting career with an average starting pay of $45,000 and receive an average 2.5% increase annually. We assume you will contribute 4% of your pretax income to your company 401(k), and your company matches 50% of your contributions. The S&P has good years of gains and years where losses occur. On average, we will estimate that you make 10% per year. Starting at age 25 until you are 65, you'll contribute $119,500. Your employer contributes $62,500. Your nest egg for retirement is estimated to be $1,563,700. If you could increase your contributions from 4% to 10%, your nest egg for retirement in your 401(k) would be worth $3.9 million. A good rule of thumb for retirement is to take distributions of no more than 4% per year. This allows for up and down fluctuations in the market, as you are taking distributions without running out of money. With $3.9 million, a distribution of $156k sounds nice. But not so fast. Now, you have to pay taxes on that distribution. People think retirement is going to be less costly than your working years. It is true, you won't have the expenses of going to work. What do you plan on doing in retirement? Do you want to travel, golf, or have hobbies? These things all cost money. There's also healthcare. As we age, we tend to spend more on healthcare. Why plan to have just enough in retirement to get by? If you are accustomed to being in the rich class, you might find you feel like you're taking a cut in pay and having to reduce your extravagant lifestyle. I have seen couples all too often living a rich lifestyle and retiring. They don't use the 4% rule to take distributions out and end up flying through their 401(k), only to have social security to live on. Living on Social Security offers little financial freedom, let alone wealth.

This is where financial freedom comes in. An important key to gaining financial freedom is to live below your means and stay out of debt. By living below your means, you spend less than you bring home after taxes. By doing so, you have money you can add to investments. With the right investment strategies, you can have 10 million dollars in 20 years. With a ROTH IRA, you can invest after-tax money and never pay taxes on the gains. Using the example from the 401(k), your contributions end up being much less than your gains over time. I would much rather pay less taxes on the smaller amount. While there are multiple ways to add investments to create financial freedom, this book will focus on trading to obtain financial freedom.

The stock market has years of gains when the market is rising. There are also years when the market is falling, causing losses in stocks and many 401(k) accounts. Over the long run, the market tends to average a profit of 10% per year. If you talk with a financial advisor, they will not tell you they expect to make you 10% per year. You can invest in a fund that follows the S&P 500, like VOO, and make what the market makes. You will also lose what the market is losing in a downtrend. I was searching for a way to make money both when the market is going up and when the market is falling. I wanted a chance to make more than the market. This is when I learned about trading.

WHAT IS TRADING?

Trading refers to the buying and selling of financial assets, such as stocks, bonds, commodities, currencies, or other securities, to generate a profit. Traders try to make a profit by taking advantage of price changes in the market, usually in a short to medium period of time. This is characterized as active investing, as it contrasts with buy-and-hold strategies, which involve a more passive approach.

Stocks are shares of ownership in a company. When you buy stocks, you can make money in two ways: by receiving dividends (a payment to shareholders) and by increasing stock prices as the company becomes more valuable. When you buy stock, you are, in essence, becoming part-owner of the company. As part-owner, you are entitled to receive a portion of the profits. A company pays dividends to stockholders as EPS (earnings per share). If you own 100 shares of a company and the company distributes EPS of $3, you will receive $300 as your portion of the distributed earnings. Stocks are bought and sold on stock markets like the NYSE (New York Stock Exchange) or NASDAQ, which is known for tech companies. Each stock on these exchanges has a ticker symbol, a unique set of one to five letters that helps identify the stock. Think of it as an abbreviation for the company.

Examples:

AAPL = Apple Inc. (on the Nasdaq)

MSFT = Microsoft Corporation (on The Nasdaq)

TSLA = Tesla Inc. (on the Nasdaq)

WMT = Walmart (on the NYSE)

Purchasing shares of a company little by little can add up to your wealth accumulation. Some stocks are quite pricey, though, with a bid price over $1,000. However, there is a way to get the benefit of owning shares of a company for a fraction of the cost. This is done using options. Options are a way of using leverage to control stocks.

Options are a way to invest in a company's stock without paying the full purchase price of the shares. Options are issued in "lots." Regular equities are 100 shares of stock per lot. Options aren't just for stocks; they can also be traded on things like futures, natural gas, currency, bonds, metals, and more. The number of shares per lot in these can vary from 50 to 25,000. Another alternative for investing is through an ETF (exchange-traded fund). An ETF is like a big basket with different stocks, so you can invest in many companies without buying each stock individually. For example, there is an ETF for the S&P 500, called SPY, and others are focused on specific areas, like real estate, technology, banking, healthcare, etc.

Options trading involves two types of options you will learn about in detail in the next chapter:

Calls and **Puts**

A **call** option is the right to buy a stock at a specific price.

A **put** option is the right to sell a stock at a specific price.

***Throughout this text, the use of "stock" or "underlying" is used interchangeably for stock, future, ETF, commodity, or underlying.

Stocks and ETFs do not have an expiration date, meaning you can hold shares as long as you like. This buy-and-hold is the way of a passive investor. Options, on the other hand, are a part of active investing. Active investing does not mean you have to watch your trade all day. As an active investor, you'll want to check your trade positions anywhere from once daily to once every two weeks, depending on your strategies. Options have an expiration date based on the date you select. The price of an option is a small percentage of the stock's price. To start investing in stocks or options, you'll need to open a brokerage account. Do your research to find the best platform for you. Personally, I use Tastytrade for most of my accounts. But this is just my preference, and not a recommendation. I like it because it is easy to use, especially for quick, simple trades, but what works for me may not work for you. I use Thinkorswim for other accounts. I like the technical analysis tools on their platform. When you open a brokerage account, you can search for an underlying that you are interested in. We will use Amazon as an example with the ticker symbol AMZN. Once you log in to your brokerage platform, you'll enter the ticker symbol to pull up the stock, and the page will look something like this.

Different brokerages may look slightly different, but they all show the same key information. You'll see two important prices near the ticker symbol: the Bid (sell price) and the Ask (buy price). If you want to buy or sell a stock, you'll click on either the Bid or Ask price at his point. If you want to trade options, below the ticker symbol, you'll find the options chain, which lists the available options contracts for that stock. The dates in the list of options chains are the expiration dates. Your choice of expiration dates for an option can vary. Most stocks have options that expire on the third Friday of every month. These are referred to as monthly options. Some stocks also offer weekly options, which expire on other Fridays. The number of days from when you place your trade to the expiration date is called "DTE," or days to expiration. Indices like SPX (S&P 200) and NDX (Nasdaq), as well as the corresponding ETF and futures, trade daily and offer 0 DTE options. For example, if you're looking at a contract that expires on February 14, and it shows "36d," this means there are 36 days left until the expiration (DTE). Some investors like to choose long-term options, but others prefer shorter ones to reduce risk from binary events (a known event that can cause an extreme move in stock price). There is considerable agreement that using the expiration closest to 45 DTE is a sweet spot. Some platforms will have a line between dates with an "E." The purple line in the above example with the "E" shows when the company will report earnings. This is helpful if you want to avoid trading around earnings. You could select a date before earnings or wait until after earnings to place your trade. By clicking on an expiration date in the options chain, you will see the individual strike prices you have to choose from.

TABLE CURVE ACTIVE GRID CRYPTO PAIRS ANALYSIS STOCK LONG GO ALL

Feb 14, 2025

Open Int	Delta	Bid (Sell)	Ask (Buy)	Strike	Bid (Sell)	Ask (Buy)	Delta	Open Int
		Calls	36d		Puts			
48	0.74	21.15	22.45	205	3.40	3.60	-0.21	204
23	0.68	17.70	18.40	210	4.60	5.00	-0.30	122
95	0.62	14.05	14.95	215	6.35	6.75	-0.37	138
92	0.54	11.35	11.85	220	8.25	8.75	-0.46	93
119	0.47	8.85	9.35	225	10.65	11.25	-0.54	39
227	0.39	6.80	7.20	230	13.40	14.25	-0.62	125
968	0.32	4.95	5.40	235	15.85	18.40	-0.71	110
347	0.26	3.65	3.85	240	19.10	22.10	-0.73	1
490	0.20	2.60	2.99	245	22.40	26.20	-0.85	0

In the example above, AMZN is trading at $222.12, so 100 shares would cost $22,212. However, one lot of call options on AMZN at the 225 strike price with an expiration date of February 14 is $910. The strike price is the price you select for the option you wish to purchase or sell. This is also referred to as the exercise price. I will go into more detail shortly. One lot of options for Feb 14 is like controlling 100 shares of AMZN until February 14 for less than 5% of the cost. This is called leverage, which means controlling a large amount of stock for a small percentage of cash.

If AMZN rises 100 points before February 14:

	cost to carry	Profit est.		
If you owned shares	$22,312	$10,000	45%	Gain on Stocks
If you bought options	$910	~$9,000	1099%	Gain on Options

If you look at the chart for AMZN, you can see how leverage works. Trading options can give you nearly the same profit as buying stocks. However, because of leverage, your return on investment (ROI) is more than 20 times greater. Let's think of it this way: imagine you have $25,000 to invest in stocks. You could buy 100 shares of AMZN. But if you decide to use options, you could buy 25 option lots for $22,750. This would let you control 2,500 shares of AMZN. With the 100 shares of stock, your profit would be $10,000, but with the 25 lots of options, your profit would be nearly $250,000. That's the power of leverage!

Options are the best way to leverage a small amount of risk capital into potentially massive returns. With options, you can grow a small account faster than you could by just buying stocks, and you don't need a lot of money to start trading options.

What about risk?

When you purchase stock, you make money in two ways: by receiving dividends and by selling the stock at a higher price once the price has increased. However, if the stock price decreases, you lose money by selling at a lower price than you paid. If you don't sell and the stock price starts to rise again, you don't lose anything. However, some stocks can reach an all-time high, fall lower, and take quite a long time to reach the high again. If you bought the stock at its highest point, you might have to wait a while to make money on it. Stocks are affected by many market events, like earnings reports, which happen every quarter. These reports can cause big changes in a stock's price. Sometimes, a company might be doing well, but if something in the earnings report scares investors, the stock price can drop. This up-and-down movement can make it feel like you are taking one step forward and one step back. This is especially true for stocks trading up and down within a range for an extended period. This extended period is called consolidation. When people talk about the stock market, they usually mean the S&P 500, an index that tracks the performance of 500 of the biggest companies on US stock exchanges.

Over time, the market goes through uptrend, consolidation, and downtrend cycles. About 50% to 60% of the time, the market is in a consolidation phase, which means it's moving up and down within a certain range instead of going steadily higher or lower.

A candlestick chart shows the price movement for the timeframe you are looking for. If you are looking at a daily candlestick chart. Each candle reflects the movement for one day. A red candle indicates the price closed on the day lower than where it started the day. When the market opened, the price was at the top of the square body. Price moves up and down throughout the day. The top wick reflects price movement above the opening price. However, the price falls to the bottom of the lower wick and back up again, finishing the day at the bottom of the square.

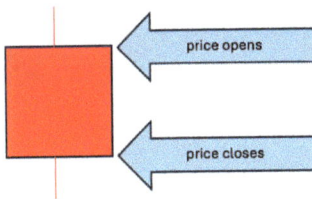

price opens

price closes

The green candle is opposite the red candle. It represents the price closing higher than the start of the day.

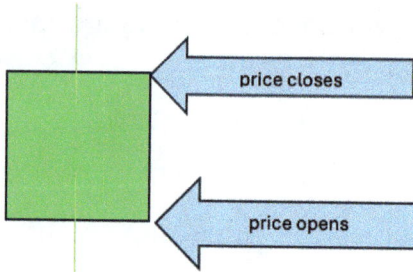

Pictured below is a candlestick chart using red and white candles.

This candlestick chart shows the price action on a daily time frame for 9 months. This means one day is represented by one candle. You can customize the look of the candles in your charts. Some prefer to use green for an up candle. A red candle indicates the price closed lower than the opening price. The opening price of a red candle is at the top of the candle's body, and the closing price is at the bottom of the body. The lines above or below the candle (called "tails") show the price movement higher or lower than the opening and closing prices. A white candle indicates the price closed higher than the opening price. The opening price on the white candle is at the bottom of the body, and the closing price is at the top of the body. In this example, the stock is in an uptrend, which you can tell because the price is moving higher from left to right. The boxed areas show periods of consolidation, where the stock moves up and down within a certain range. The top line of the box is called the "resistance line," where the price often reaches and then bounces back down. The bottom line of the box is the "support line," where the price tends to bounce back up. If you had bought the stock in mid-September at $62, expecting it to continue an uptrend, you would have had to wait until the last week of October for the price to reach that level again and break out of the consolidation. One risk of owning stocks is that you could lose money if the stock starts to go into a downtrend. You might also experience periods where your money doesn't grow because the stock is stuck in a consolidation phase.

With options, you can make money when the stock increases, decreases, or stays in range, depending on the type of trade you place. Since options have an expiration date, you can plan your trade around important events, like earnings reports or other events that might impact the stock. These events are called binary events, which can cause a stock or even the whole market to make a large move in one direction or the other. Examples of binary events include a company's earnings report or a change in leadership, like a new CEO or CFO. Events that affect the entire market, like the Federal Reserve's interest rate decisions, the Federal Open Market Committee's (FOMC) meeting notes, jobless claims, or other government announcements, are also considered binary events. You can locate the market binary events online. Many websites list events on the "US economic calendar," often showing which events are expected to cause big movements in the market. If you search for the US economic calendar, you will find many sites that list upcoming events. Your brokerage platform will also give you information about the dividends and earnings dates. While dividends usually don't cause big changes in a stock's price, it is still good to be aware of them.

OPTIONS

Options fall into two categories: American and European. This determines when an option contract can be exercised, not where the option is from. An American option can be exercised at any time between the date the options are bought or sold and the expiration date. A European option can only be exercised at expiration. Most options are American, but European-style options are usually found on indexes because they don't involve physical assignments. These indices have their own special European-style options:

BKX

DJX

HGX

NDX

OSX

RUI

RUT

SPX

UTY

VIX

XSP

Did you know that about 70% of options end up worthless? A good way to understand the concept of options expiring worthless and being exercised is to think of it like an insurance contract. If you are buying options, it's like you are buying an insurance contract. If you sell options, it's like you are acting as the insurance company to sell insurance to the insured. The premium you sell the option for is like the insurance premium an insurance company would collect for the insurance contract. I like to look at it like hurricane insurance. The closer you are to a chance of hurricane, the higher your insurance will be. With the options, the closer the strike price is to the actual price of the underlying, the more expensive the option will be. If a hurricane doesn't reach your home, no claim is made on your insurance. The insurance company keeps the amount of premium you paid as the contract expires for the duration and another premium is collected for the next duration. In the case of options, the premium collected is the profit to the seller of the option when the price of the underlying does not come in contact with the option strike price and does not get exercised. In this case the option expires worthless.

The market has a trend, which is the direction in which it is moving. The trend can be Bullish, Bearish, or Neutral.

Bullish - Think of a "bull run." Bullish means you expect the market, or a stock, to rise.

Bearish - Think of "bears sleeping, or lying down." Bearish means you expect the market or a stock to fall or go down.

A significant portion of the time, the market trades in a range, neither rising nor falling significantly, which is referred to as consolidation or neutrality.

Options involve Calls and Puts. The purpose of the call or put depends on whether you are the option's buyer or seller.

	PUT	CALL
BUYER	RIGHT TO SELL	RIGHT TO BUY
SELLER	OBLIGATION TO BUY	OBLIGATION TO SELL

Most of the strategies I discuss in this book are geared toward selling options, as selling options increases the probability of a winning trade. The definitions of calls and puts are provided from the seller's perspective.

Puts

When you sell a put, you are making a contract, like an insurance contract, which gives the buyer the right to sell you

100 stock shares at the option's strike price between now and the date of expiration. Think of it as "putting" the shares on you. As the seller, you are obligated to buy the shares at the stock price. Most options contracts issued expire worthless and are not exercised. For example, if you are selling a put option on a $100 stock with a strike price of $75, the buyer will not want to sell their shares to you at $75 when they can get $100 on the market. However, if the stock price falls to $50, it would benefit the buyer to exercise their right to sell. In this case, you would be obligated to buy the shares at $75. You could immediately sell the shares at a $25 loss or hold them, hoping the stock will rebound.

Calls

A call gives the buyer the right to buy stock at the strike price at any time between now and expiration. As the seller of a call option, you are obligated to sell the stock if the option is exercised. Think of this as having your shares "called" away. Like the put option, the buyer of the call option will only exercise their right if the stock price has risen above the strike price. For example, let's say you sell a call option for a $100 stock with a strike price of $150. The buyer of the option would not exercise at $150 when they can buy the shares on the market at $100. However, if the stock price rises to $175, the buyer would likely exercise their option. If you are the seller of the call option exercised in this case, you would have

2 options. If you own 100 shares of the stock, you will have to sell those shares at the strike price. If you do not own the shares, your loss would equal the cost of the shares on the market minus the strike price you receive and the premium you collected.

Bullish, Bearish, or Neutral?

How you use calls and puts depends on your outlook on the stock. Are you bullish, bearish, or neutral (expecting little movement)?

If you are **bullish**, you look to make a bullish trade:

Sell Puts - Expecting the price to remain above the put strike price.

Buy Calls - Expecting the price to rise above the call strike price.

If you are **Bearish**, you look to make a bearish trade:

Sell Calls - Expecting the price to remain below the call strike price.

Buy Puts - Expecting the price to fall below the put strike price.

	CALL	PUT
BUY	Assumption: Price will Rise	Assumption: Price will fall
SELL	Assumption: Price will stay the same or fall	Assumption: Price will stay the same or Rise

When you buy or sell an option, you pick a strike price, which is the target price and possible exercise of the option. The premium is the amount you pay to buy an option or the amount you receive for selling an option. On a brokerage platform, options are listed by expiration date, with calls on one side and puts on the other. One column shows the "bid," while the other shows the "ask." The bid is the sell price, and the ask is the buy price. Generally, the market price is mid-priced between the bid and ask price. The **fill price** is the price at which a market maker executes the option order.

Moneyness of an Option

CALLS					Strikes: 10		PUTS				
Extrinsic	Open.int	Delta	Bid X	Ask X	Exp	Strike	Bid X	Ask X	Extrinsic	Open.int	Delta
> 21 FEB 25 (1) 100											26.73% (±3.159)
v 21 MAR 25 (29) 100											21.14% (±11.85)
-.12	0	1.00	48.10	49.30	21 MAR 25	200	0	1.25	.625	0	-.04
-.07	0	1.00	38.20	39.30	21 MAR 25	210	0	.50	.25	1	-.03
.18	1	1.00	26.60	29.40	21 MAR 25	220	.20	.70	.45	44	-.05
.98	4	.93	18.10	19.50	21 MAR 25	230	.70	1.00	.85	6	-.11
3.68	339	.71	10.30	12.70	21 MAR 25	240	2.35	2.80	2.575	37	-.27
4.70	337	.47	4.20	5.20	21 MAR 25	250	4.60	6.80	3.52	7	-.54
1.475	571	.20	1.15	1.80	21 MAR 25	260	13.10	14.90	1.82	3	-.75
.40	8	.07	.30	.50	21 MAR 25	270	21.60	24.00	.62	1	-.88
.25	3	.04	0	.50	21 MAR 25	280	31.30	34.40	.77	0	-.89
.75	1	.07	0	1.50	21 MAR 25	290	41.40	44.70	.87	0	-.89

The Moneyness of an option refers to its position relative to the stock price. As an important distinction to recognize, moneyness does not relate to the profit or loss of a position.

o **ATM (At the money)** - at or near the closest possible position to stock price.

o **OTM (Out of the money)** - stock price has not passed the option's strike price. You want the option to be OTM as it nears expiration if you sold the option.

o **ITM (In the money)** - stock price has passed the option's strike price. You want the option to be ITM if you bought the option.

Remember, you want the option to be ITM if you bought the option and OTM if you sold it.

In the above example, the current price is 247.82. You will see a change in the shading on the calls and puts where the current price is located on the center row of strike prices. The calls are listed on the left, and the puts are listed on the right. The change in the shading is ATM. The shaded section for calls is ITM because the stock price is above the call price. Similarly, the shaded section of puts on the right side is ITM because the stock price is below the put price. You will notice in some of the examples that the strike prices are listed incrementally up, while some are incrementally down. You can change the direction your stikes are listed by clicking on the strike column for your preference.

Buying Calls and Puts

When you buy a call, you pay a premium upfront and receive the right to buy 100 shares of the underlying stock at the strike price from the day you buy the Call until the expiration date.

When you buy a put, you pay a premium upfront and receive the right to sell 100 shares of the underlying stock at the strike price from the day you buy the put up until the expiration date.

A call option becomes more valuable as the stock price rises. A put option becomes more valuable as the stock price falls.

If you buy an option, you hope its value will increase before expiration, so you can sell it for a higher price than you paid.

The premium you pay to buy an option is the maximum you can lose on the trade.

If you sell an option, you are acting like an insurance company that has sold a policy and hopes no claim will be made. If the option remains OTM, it expires worthless, and you keep the premium just like an insurance company with no claims. As the stock price moves further OTM, the option loses value. In selling an option, you intend for it to lose value to keep the premium. Since options have an expiration date, they lose time value the closer they get to expiration, and premium decay accelerates closer to expiration.

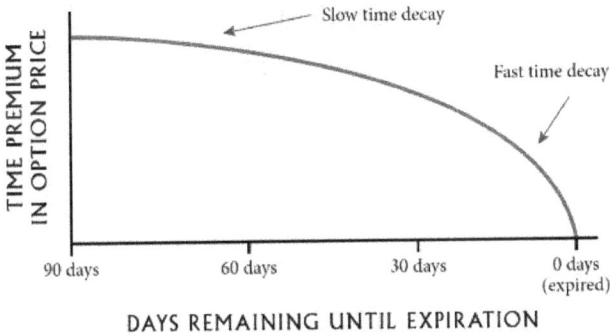

DAYS REMAINING UNTIL EXPIRATION

In the chart for a 90-day to expiration (DTE) option, time decay remains fairly consistent for most of the duration. However, once you reach 30 DTE, time decay accelerates.

When you get both the timing and direction right, you can profit quickly.

The **premium** you pay for the option has two components contributing to its value.

Option Premium = Intrinsic Value + Extrinsic Value

Extrinsic value is time value. Think of it as external (time). This is why Extrinsic value decays as time passes. Premium decay and time decay are the same thing. Extrinsic value will always be worth ZERO at expiration.

Intrinsic value is only on options that are ITM. It is the difference between the strike price and the stock price when the option is ITM.

Suppose you purchased a call option at a $75 strike price. This gives you the right to buy the stock at $75 any time before expiration. If the stock is trading at $70, you would not want to exercise your right to purchase at $75 since you can purchase the stock for less on the market. At this point, the option only has time value (extrinsic). However, if the stock price rises to $80, you now have the right to buy the stock at

$75 and sell it at $80 for a $5 profit per share. The $5 difference between the market price and the strike price is intrinsic value. The further ITM the option is, the more valuable it becomes.

A Call option has intrinsic value when the stock price is above the call strike. Intrinsic value of Call = stock price - call strike.

A Put option has intrinsic value when the stock price is below the put strike. The intrinsic value of Put = put strike - stock price.

Factors Affecting Option Value

Factor impacting intrinsic value:

1. THE UNDERLYING STOCK PRICE

Factors that impact extrinsic value (time value):

2. IMPLIED VOLATILITY

3. TIME TO EXPIRATION (EXPIRY)

4. DIVIDENDS

5. INTEREST RATES

If you buy options, you pay a debit for the premium. You expect the price to move in your favor. For calls, you want the stock price to go up. For puts, you want the stock price to go down.

The opposite is true for selling options. You will collect a credit for the premium. If you sell a call, you want the stock price to remain below the call strike (OTM), so it expires worthless. If the stock price falls, the call option loses value. If you sell a put, you want the stock price to remain above the put strike (OTM), causing the option to lose value as the stock price rises.

When you are investing in the stock market, the goal is always to buy low, sell high. So, if the stock you are looking at is high and you feel it is overpriced and do for a pullback, you would short the stock. In other words you would sell the stock at a high price with hopes of buying it back to close your position when the stock drops. The same is true with options. If you are buying options, the goal is to buy the option when it is low and sell when the option increases in value. When selling options, you are selling high and buying to close the position when the option price has decreased in value.

FACTORS AFFECTING OPTION PRICING

The stock price is the only factor that impacts the intrinsic value of an option. If the stock price is in-the-money (ITM), the option's value will increase based on how far the stock moves in the money. When buying options, it is done for a debit. If we buy a call option, we want the stock price to rise. The higher the stock price climbs, the more value is added to the call option. This creates intrinsic value when the stock price moves ITM. If we buy a put, we want the price to decrease. The further the stock price falls, the more value is added to the put option.

The opposite is true when selling options. If we sell a call, we want the stock price to remain below the strike price of the call (out-of-the-money, OTM) and for the option to expire worthless. If the stock price falls, the option loses value. We want the stock price to remain above the put strike (OTM) when selling a put. A put loses value as the stock price rises.

IMPLIED VOLATILITY (IV)

A rise in implied volatility (IV) will lead to an increase in the value of an option. Implied volatility is the estimated future volatility of a stock's price. IV provides a one standard deviation expected move over the next 12 months. One standard deviation means that, statistically and based on volatility, the price is likely to stay within this range approximately 68% of the time. One standard deviation is written as 1σ. The price is expected to remain in a 2σ range about 95% of the time and a 3σ range about 99.7% of the time. A higher IV – a more significant expected movement in price - means the future path of a stock is expected to be more uncertain. IV does not indicate direction. It will not tell you whether a stock is expected to rise or fall, only the magnitude of the potential price fluctuation. IV reflects the market's emotional perception of the future price of the underlying asset, as expressed in the option's price.

For example:

A stock trading at 100 with an IV of .10 or 10%, is expected to move up or down by approximately 10% over the next 12 months. This expected move falls within a 1σ range.

You can calculate the expected move within 1σ by using a formula:

$$1\sigma \text{ expected range } (\%) = \text{IV} \times \sqrt{\text{\# of days of trade} \div 365}$$

Or

$$1\sigma \text{ expected range (\$)} = \text{stock price x IV x } \sqrt{\text{\# of days of trade} \div 365}$$

For simplicity, calculations for a 45 DTE (days to expiration) often use $\sqrt{(45 \div 365)} \sim 0.35$ for ease of calculation.

Another example:

You are looking at TSLA (Tesla), which is trading at 396. The IV (not to be confused with IVR) is 64% for a one-year expiration. You can find this by checking the options chain one year out.

The calculation for 45 DTE would be 396 x 0.64 x 0.35 = 88.99. In other words, the 1σ range is from 484.99 to 301.01. This range is often shown on the platform with a dotted line to represent 1σ expected move, so you don't need to calculate it manually.

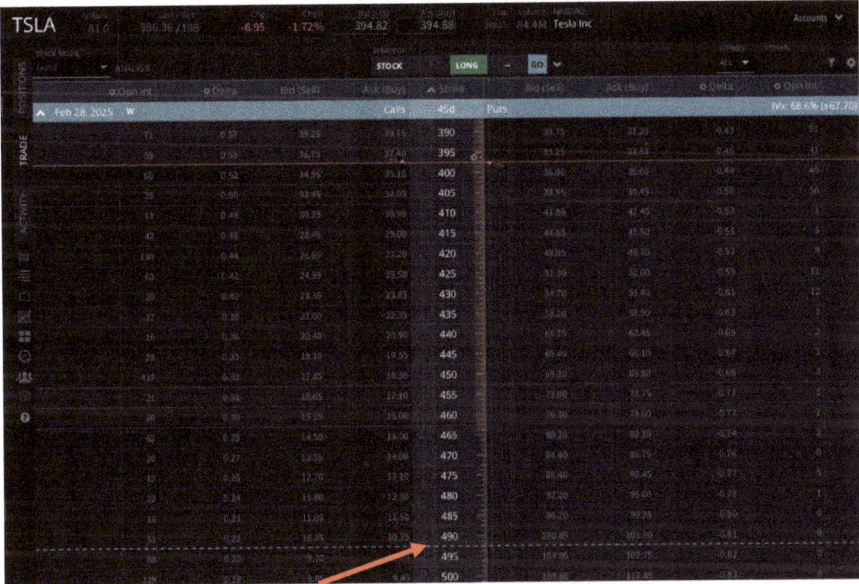

The image above shows the 1σ dotted line to the upside on the platform between the 490 and 495 strikes. The 2σ range is displayed further out, using a wider dotted line to indicate the more expansive range.

Back-of-the-envelope methods for calculating expected move involve using the premiums:

(ATM Call + ATM Put + first OTM Call + first OTM Put) ÷ 2

or

(ATM Call + ATM Put) x 0.85

An even easier way to estimate expected move is to look for the delta 25 to 30 calls and puts with high open interest. These will approximate the expected move.

Options price is driven more by IV than by the price of the underlying stock. IV can fluctuate based on the price change of the underlying as well as shifts in market perception. A higher IV results in a higher options price. This is why traders look at IV rank (IVR). Options on stocks with a higher IVR tend to have higher premiums, making them more favorable for selling strategies. IV typically contracts after a sharp increase, reducing the value of options and generating profits for those who sold options for a premium when IV was high.

IV is positively correlated with an option's value. Higher IV increases the extrinsic value for both calls and puts. In general, IV rises when the market is bearish and falls when the market is bullish. Therefore, IV is inversely correlated with the stock price: when a stock rallies, IV typically declines; when a stock experiences a sell-off or pull-back, IV usually rises.

Even with different time frames, you can still calculate expected moves:

For example: an option has 90 days to expiry, IV of 20% and the underlying stock price is $50

$$1 \, SD = \sqrt{90/365} * 0.20 * \$50$$

$1SD = \$4.97$

- Over the next 90 days, the stock would have a 68.2% chance of rising or falling by $4.97 (trading range of $45.03 to $54.97)

IV estimates a one standard deviation move, which encompasses 68.2% of all possible outcomes. In other words, IV provides an estimate of the range within which a stock is expected to trade over a given period, with a 68.2% probability.

The **VIX** is the CBOE's volatility index, reflecting the market's expectations for forward-looking 30-day volatility. It is calculated using the implied volatilities of a wide range of S&P 500 options. The VIX serves as a general barometer of overall stock market volatility. However, it is not a leading indicator - it only reflects current market conditions. Spikes in the VIX occur as the market is falling, but they do not predict future declines.

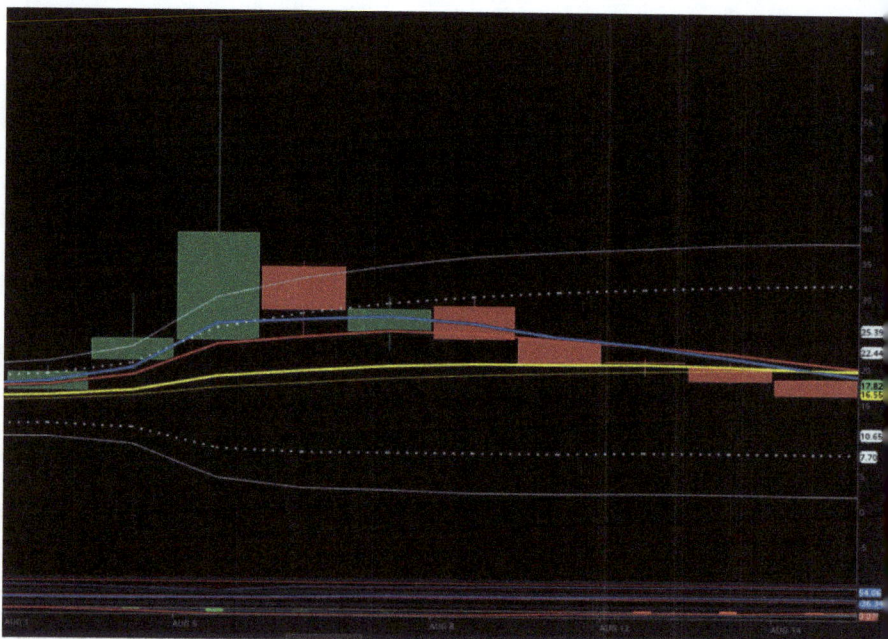

A VIX reading 25 represents an expected annual change in the S&P 500 of +/- 25%, with 68% confidence. To estimate the expected range for one month, divide the VIX by $\sqrt{12}$ to get the expected range for 1 month.

VIX READINGS

- < 20 Relaxed bull market

- at 20 neutral market

- 20 to 40 is an anxious market

- 40 is generally a bear market with high anxiety

When deciding which options to buy or sell, consider the IVR (Implied Volatility Rank). IVR compares the current IV to its range over the past 52 weeks and ranks the current IV between 0 and 100. This reflects its relative position between the yearly high and low.

How is IVR Calculated?

$$IV\,rank = \frac{current\ IV - 52\ week\ IV\,low}{52\ week\ IV\,high - 52\ week\ IV\,low} \times 100$$

A stock with an IVR above 50 will typically have higher option premiums.

TIME TO EXPIRATION (EXPIRY)

The greater the time to expiration, the more expensive the option.

More time means more extrinsic value.

DIVIDENDS

Dividends are generally a non-event. This means it is an event that usually will not affect the movement of the stock price going up or down by much. When a stock pays a dividend, its share price typically falls by the dividend amount. Dividends usually cause only a minor fluctuation in price.

INTEREST RATES

Interest rates are another non-event. Rising interest rates mildly increase the value of calls and slightly decrease the value of puts. However, this usually does not affect a short-term directional options trader.

THE "GREEKS"

Five "Greeks" are mainly used to measure the impact of various factors on the price of an option.

DELTA

Delta measures the impact of a change in the price of the underlying stock. Call options have a positive delta, ranging from 0 to 1. Put options have a negative delta, ranging from

0 to -1. Delta states how much an option price is expected to change given a $1.00 change in the stock price.

For example, if a call option has a delta of 0.5 (also expressed as "delta 50" or "50 Δ"), a $1 rise in the stock price would increase the option's value by $0.50.

A put option with a delta of -0.30 will increase in value by $0.30 for every $1 the price falls. The higher the delta, the greater the sensitivity to stock price changes. An option with 1Δ will move $1 for every $1 change in the stock price.

Delta also reflects the moneyness of an option.

calls and puts with 50 Δ are ATM

> 50 Δ are ITM

< 50 Δ are OTM

Options with > 50 Δ are more expensive because they are ITM and therefore have intrinsic value and extrinsic value. Options =< 50Δ only have extrinsic value.

Another way to think about delta is in terms of equivalent share exposure:

a call with 70 Δ has a "delta-adjusted" exposure to 70 shares - effectively being long 70 shares. A put at 30 Δ is equivalent to being short 30 shares.

Another way to look at delta is the probability that the option will be ITM at expiration. A 60 Δ option has approximately a 60% chance of being ITM at expiration. Similarly, A call with a 30 Δ would have roughly a 30% chance of expiring ITM.

The goal when buying options is for them to expire ITM. When selling options, the objective is for them to remain OTM.

When using delta for selling options, a 60 Δ has roughly a 40% chance of expiring OTM.

o Delta	o Opn Int	Mid Pr	:lta	B
2025 W /ESH5 (E2B)		✓ Delta		
0.78	0	Theta	).78	
0.76	0	Gamma	).76	
0.74	0	Vega	).74	
0.72	0	Opn Int	).72	
0.69	0	Volm	).69	
0.66	41	ITM %	).66	
0.63	0	OTM %	).63	
0.60	0	Touch %	).60	
0.56	0	Impl Vol	).56	
0.53	1	Int	).53	
		Ext		

Options chains include a column that can be customized to your preferences. You can choose to display metrics such as Delta, ITM%, OTM%, Probability of Touch %, and many others.

THETA

Theta measures the impact of time decay – how much an option's extrinsic value decreases each day due to the passage of time, assuming the underlying price and IV remain constant. It is also known as premium decay, time decay, theta decay, or negative theta.

When you buy options, you are trading against the clock, so it's important to get the direction correct quickly to profit or benefit from an increase in IV to offset theta decay.

Time decay (theta) is less pronounced the more the option is ITM.

Buying an option ITM has a higher probability of profit than buying an option OTM. This means you have a higher chance of making money on the trade. Conversely, selling an option OTM has a higher probability of profit than selling an option ITM, as OTM options have a greater chance of expiring worthless.

A good rule of thumb when deciding where to buy an option is that the extrinsic value should not exceed one-third (33%) of the total option premium.

OTHER GREEKS

The other three Greeks are not used as commonly when determining strategy. However, being familiar with these terms can be helpful. GAMMA measures the rate of change of the delta. VEGA measures the sensitivity of the option's price to changes in IV. RHO measures the impact of changes in interest rates on the option's price. For our purposes, we won't be referencing these Greeks further.

WHERE DO YOU BEGIN

You are familiar with the ins and outs of options pricing now. You are ready to put your feet in the water and give trading a chance. What strike should you choose? Do you buy or sell? Do you use Puts or Calls? Here are some things to keep in mind in your selection:

• Buying an option ITM has a higher probability of profit than buying OTM.

• Selling an option OTM has a higher probability of profit than selling ITM. They have a high probability of expiring worthless.

• A good rule of thumb in deciding where to buy an option is that extrinsic value should not exceed one-third (33%) of the total option premium.

• Monthly expirations generally have more open interest. You should look for open interest of at least 100. This will make it easier to get a fill on entries and exits. At a minimum, you should see 10 open interests for every lot you want to put on.

• You want the stock to be liquid for easy entry and exit fills. Tight bid/ask spreads offer higher liquidity. A stock with a .20 spread between bid and ask is more liquid than a stock with a $10 wide spread.

• Check for earnings dates if you are trading an option on an individual stock. Anything can happen during earnings. You want to avoid stocks that have earnings within the next two weeks unless you are specifically putting on an earnings trade.

Data shows there is a sweet spot for options around 45 DTE. When you get into an option trade at 45 DTE, you want to get out of the trade at 21 DTE. You only stay in the trade for 24 days because of the acceleration of time decay closer to expiration.

You don't need to use fundamental analysis for options. You are not in the market long enough for fundamentals to come into play. Fundamental analysis is time-consuming. These days, the market has already priced fundamentals into options.

Determine if you want to place a bullish, bearish, or neutral trade. This is where a little technical analysis comes in. You don't have to have charts with loads of information on them. There is an old quote, "The trend is your friend." If the trend is up, use bullish trades. If the trend is down, use bearish trades. Trendlines can be used to do a trend analysis. Trend analysis involves examining historical price action to identify patterns or trends that can help predict future movements or outcomes. An upward trend will have price candles making higher highs and higher lows. A downtrend will have price candles making lower highs and lower lows.

A line is drawn connecting the lows in a bullish uptrend in green. When the price starts trading below that trend line and continues to move lower, a line drawn above the price action on the highs confirms a change in trend to a bearish trend.

When a stock is in a bullish trend, you will have a higher probability trade by looking for a trade entry near a pullback. In other words, you will have a higher chance of the trade being a winner. This is the case where you are looking to "buy the dip." In the previous example, you can clearly see the uptrend. When you see the price pull back to the green trend line and then begin to move back up, this is the dip signal you are looking for to enter a bullish trade. The opposite is the case in a bearish trend where you are looking to "sell the rip." The candlestick chart of price action can look choppy in some cases. The use of moving averages can smooth out the price action. Moving averages take the price over the past number of candles and average them. Such as a 13 day moving average will give the average price over the past 13 days. This would be written as "13 SMA" for the 13 day simple moving average. The following day, the last day is added, and the oldest day is not included. Specifically, an Exponential Moving Average (EMA) is a type of moving average that places more weight on recent prices, making it more responsive to new information. Using the moving averages, uptrend stocks will have the shorter dated moving averages above the longer moving average on a chart. You can use a watchlist of your favorite stocks to check for pullbacks. A watchlist is simply a list of stocks saved in a list for you to easily reference. Many platforms have preexisting watchlists for certain criteria and you can save your own personal watchlists to your liking. Some platforms have a scan function. This is a function to apply certain criteria to in order for the scanner to look through all the stocks for the ones that fit your selection criteria. I use Thinkorswim for my scans and charting. In order to scan for a stock that is in an uptrend I look for stocks with the 13 EMA above the 34 EMA. I also use the stochastic oscillator, which will be described in detail further in the chapter, to help signal a pullback. I also look for the stochastic oscillator with a setting of 8,3,3 to fall below 40. To make sure the stock is at the bottom of the pullback, you should wait for a confirmation. Look at the candle that has the lowest point on the pullback. On the candle following that closes above the highest point on the low candle, you have received confirmation. You should enter your bullish trade on the next green candle. If you are looking at a bearish trade, you would mirror the bullish trade. In other words, the 13 EMA needs to be below the 34 EMA. The stochastic oscillator should rise above 60, and the trade is involving a rise to the mean from a falling price. You are selling the rip. The candle to look for is the high candle. The confirmation candle will be the next red candle to close below the low of the high candle. You then want to enter the trade at the next red candle.

Using the scan tool is not a necessity. If you don't have a platform with that ability, you can set up a watchlist of good, liquid, stocks that have been on a long-term uptrend. The following is an example of a two-year chart on Netflix. There is an obvious uptrend with occasional pullbacks. Using stocks like this in a watchlist, you can view the charts daily to recognize a pullback and the confirmation candle after the low candle.

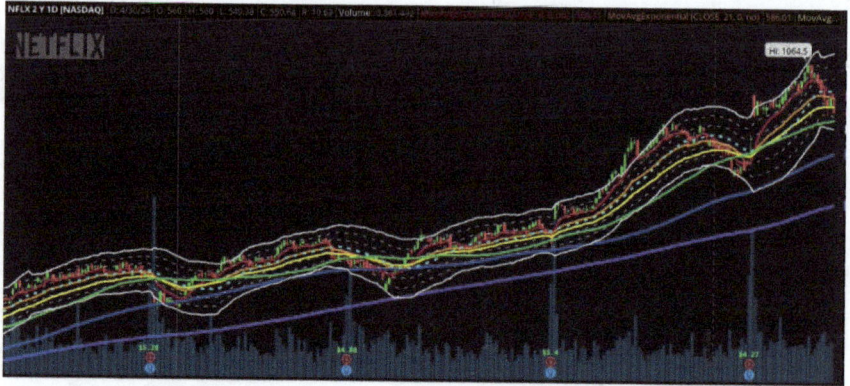

The next example is a stock you would want to avoid. It's very choppy. It goes from uptrend to downtrend back and forth in a range for an extended period. If you trade at the wrong point, you could risk a loss occurring quite quickly.

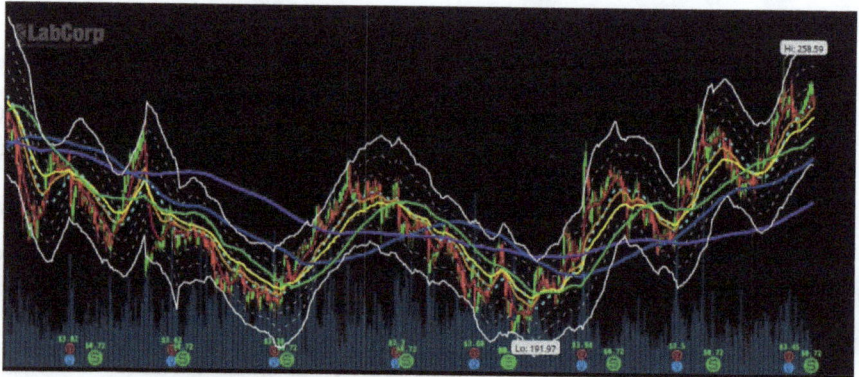

Support and resistance can be a way of deciding which way to trade. With the example given earlier above, for the trendline, the trendline can also serve as support. Support acts as a floor. This is the area where price tends to stop falling. Resistance acts as a ceiling. This is where the price tends to resist going above and tends to fall back. When the price rises above the resistance, the resistance becomes the new support. When the price drops below the support, it becomes resistance. Here is an example of typical support and resistance. The support and resistance tend to create a zone. Sometimes, the price seems to have broken resistance or support, only to retrace. This is a false breakout. You can minimize false breakouts by waiting for a confirmation. Get 1 or 2 more candlesticks out to confirm the breakout. This won't eliminate 100% of false breakouts. However, it will minimize the number. When you are trading for the dip or rip, you want to make sure the price is at support on the low point of the dip and resistance for the high point on the rip.

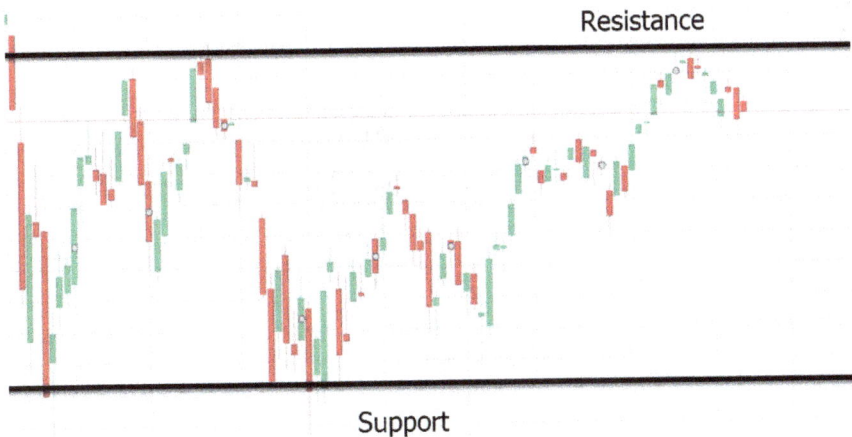

Resistance

Support

Candlestick and chart patterns can be used to determine an opinion of direction and anticipate potential movement.

Other technical indications like moving averages, stochastics, MACD, and many others can be used.

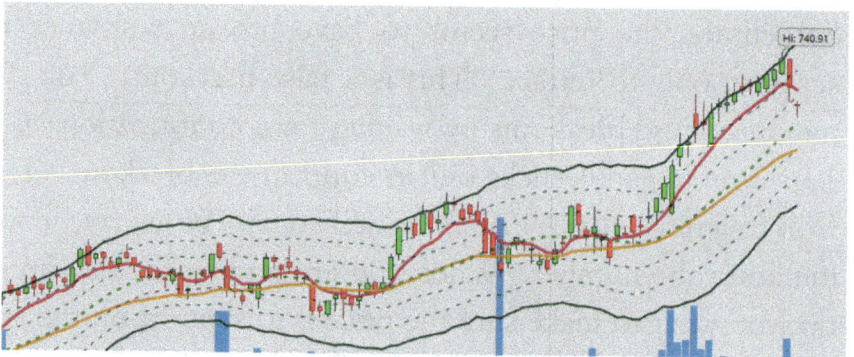

Be careful not to overload your chart with indicators. In the chart above I use two moving averages for the trend and three Keltner channels for support and resistance. Keltner Channels are a type of volatility-based technical indicator composed of three lines: 1) A middle line, typically a Simple Moving Average (commonly a 21-period SMA). 2) An upper band set at a multiple (e.g., 2x) of the Average True Range (ATR) above the SMA. And 3) A lower band set the same multiple of the ATR below the SMA.

They help traders identify overbought/oversold conditions, trend direction, and potential breakout points. Unlike Bollinger Bands, which use standard deviation, Keltner Channels use ATR to measure volatility. Average True Range (ATR) is a technical indicator that measures market volatility. It is commonly used in trading to gauge how much an asset typically moves over a given time period. The Keltner channels are set up with 1, 2, and 3 ATRs. The center line for the Keltner channels is the 21 SMA. The 21 SMA represents the mean. The price will usually pullback or pullup to the mean. Look to enter your trade within 1 ATR of the mean. You can look at the history of the stock and see how it will react before making a pullback. Some stocks will go to 2 ATRs before turning back. Some will go to 3. Keep this in mind when deciding when to the take profits and get out of the trade. You can see in the above example at some points the price hugs the top of 3 ATRs for some time. Don't try to stay in too long and end up in a pullback giving back profits. Be mechanical and take your profits. You can get back in on the next pullback.

Price action is choppy when you see plenty of pullbacks. Most stocks don't go up every day for an extended time. They have sudden pullbacks.

Moving Averages smooth out the price action and filter the noise of the random short-term price moves, revealing the underlying trend.

Exponential moving averages (EMAs) highlight short to medium-term trends. Simple moving averages (SMAs) identify medium to long-term trends.

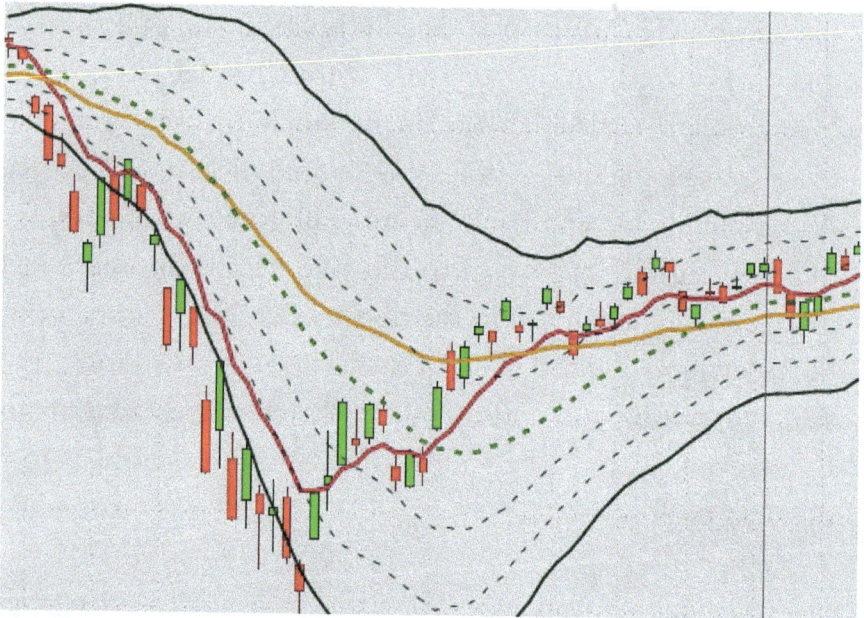

This is a weekly chart during the 2020 COVID-19 crash. The heavy red line is the 8 EMA. The heavy yellow line is the 34 EMA. When the price fell below the 34 EMA, a signal of

change in the trend occurred. The 8 EMA then crossed below
the 34 EMA.

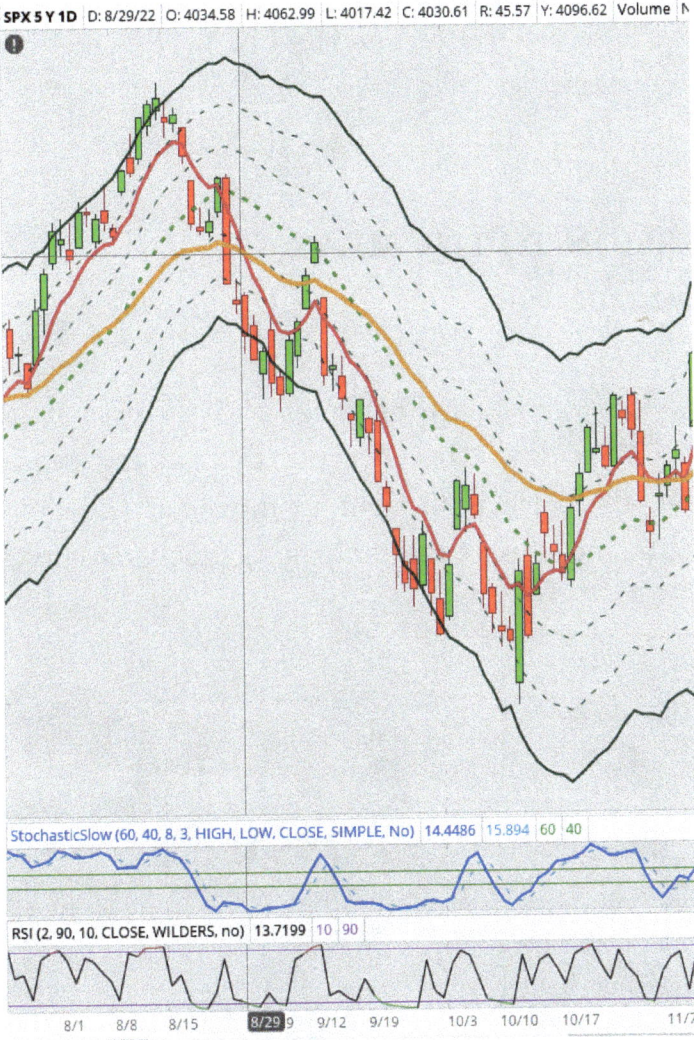

Look how quickly the change in trend can be spotted on
SPX in 2022 as it moves into a bear market. In August 2022,
there was a pullback just above the 34 EMA. It did not cross

it. Then a few days later it does, and the 8 EMA crossed below the 34 EMA, confirming the bear market. Sometimes, I switch to the 8 EMA and 21 EMA for individual stocks. In choppy markets, I will also use 13 EMA and 24 EMA. It's a matter of personal preference.

REVERSION TO THE MEAN

The 21 SMA is generally the average price the stock traded for the past 21 trading days. Because the moving average smooths out, the price is thought to move up and down, reverting to the mean like a rubber band is attached to it.

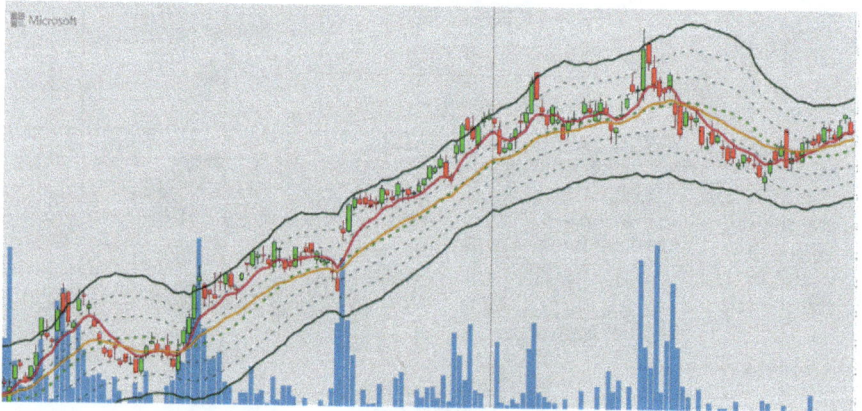

The example above is a chart on MSFT (Microsoft). The heavy yellow line in the middle is the 21 SMA. This represents the mean. You can see how the price rises above and falls below, mostly hovering around the mean. The way to set up your chart to see the mean with the channels is by using Keltner Channels. I use three Keltner channels. I have the length on each one set at 21 days with the average type of "SIMPLE." On the first channel, I set a factor of 3.0; on the second channel, I set a factor of 2.0. The last channel will have a factor of 1.0. You can use these channels as an estimate of when you feel the stock is over-extended (near the top of the channel) or near the bottom of the channel and due for a pull-back to the mean. Sometimes, the stock will ride up or down, hugging the outer band before reverting to the mean.

Another indicator I use is the MACD (Moving Average Convergence Divergence), which consists of three parts and is used to gauge momentum. The MACD consists of 3 parts:

1. MACD Line: The difference between two exponential moving averages (EMA).

2. Signal Line: This is a 9-period EMA of the MACD line itself. It smooths the MACD line to identify signals more clearly.

3. MACD Histogram: This represents the difference between the MACD line and the Signal line. It visually displays the relationship between them.

There are three things to consider when looking at the MACD. Check for crossovers, divergence, and zero-line crosses.

When the MACD and Signal lines crossover, this is your primary signal.

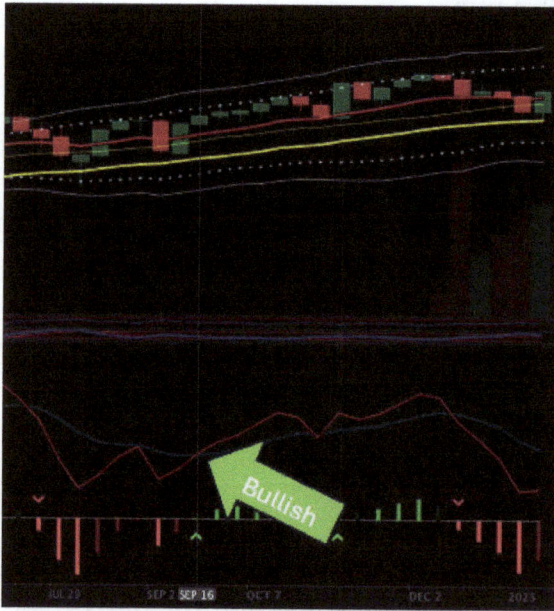

MACD line crosses above the Signal line. This is a bullish signal indicating potential upward momentum.

MACD crosses below the Signal line. This is a bearish signal indicating potential downward momentum. You can see in the example above that just as the events leading up to the August 5 volatility spike, the MACD gave a bearish signal.

Divergence occurs when the price action and MACD move in opposite directions. A potential price reversal is signaled when the price makes lower lows while the MACD makes higher lows. This is a bullish divergence. An indication of a potential price reversal to the downside is signaled when the price is making higher highs while the MACD is making lower highs. This is a bearish divergence.

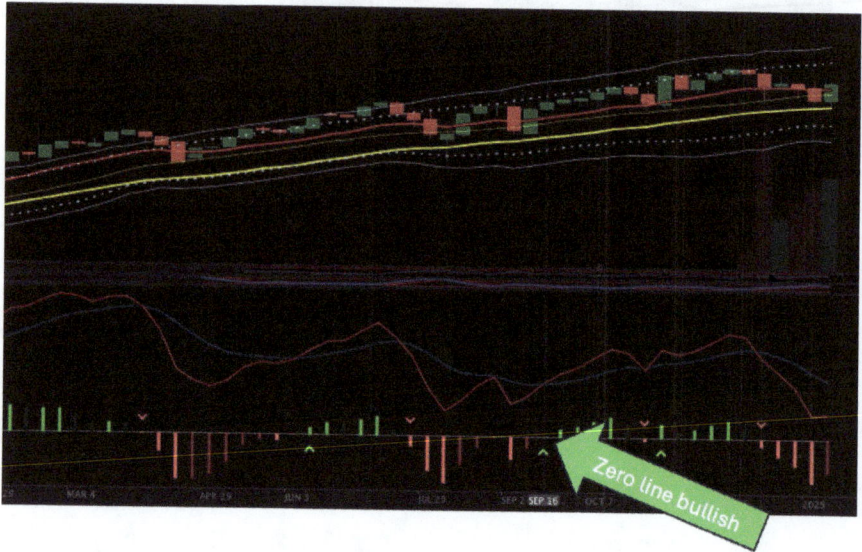

Zero Line crossing refers to the MACD line crossing above or below the zero line. A bullish signal is given when the MACD line crosses above the zero line. A bearish signal is given when the MACD line crosses below the zero line.

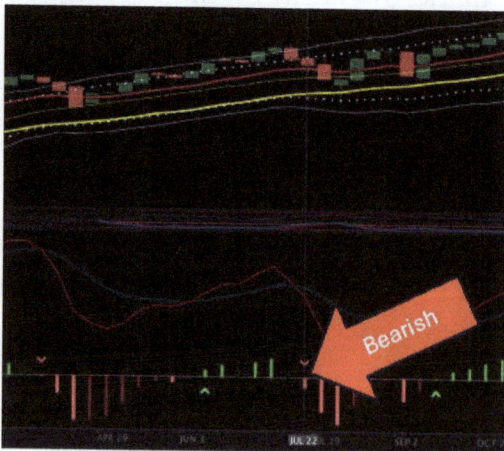

The settings on the MACD of (12, 26, 9) are widely used. I have found the settings I prefer to use are (8, 12, 9). The MACD indicator is a lagging indicator because it reacts to price changes after they have occurred, which can sometimes lead to late signals. MACD helps identify trends, momentum, and potential reversals when used with other indicators.

The Slow Stochastic is a technical indicator used to gauge the momentum of price movement. It compares a stock's closing price to its price range over a period. The indicator consists of two lines: Fast Stochastic (%K) and Slow Stochastic (%D).

- %K   This line represents the percentage of the closing price relative to the highest high and lowest low over a specified period (usually 14 days). The formula used to calculate %K is [(Current Close – Lowest Low) / (Highest High – Lowest Low)] *100.

- %D   This line is a moving average of the %K line, usually over a 3-day period.

The Slow Stochastic indicator oscillates between 0 and 100, with readings above 80 indicating overbought conditions and readings below 20 indicating oversold conditions. Here are some common ways to interpret the Slow Stochastic:

Bullish signals:

- When %K crosses above %D, it's a buy signal.

- When the indicator falls below 20 and then rises above it, it's a bullish signal.

Bearish signals:

- When %K crosses below %D, it's a sell signal.

- When the indicator rises above 80 and then falls below it, it's a bearish signal.

Divergences:

- When the indicator makes a lower high while the price makes a higher high, it's a bearish divergence.

- When the indicator makes a higher low while the price makes a lower low, it's a bullish divergence.

There are key differences between Fast and Slow Stochastic. The Fast Stochastic (%K) is more sensitive to price movements, while the Slow Stochastic (%D) is smoother and less sensitive. The Slow Stochastic is more helpful in identifying trends, while the Fast Stochastic is better for spotting short-term reversals.

Like the other indicators, the Slow Stochastic is not foolproof and should be used in conjunction with other analyses. It can produce false signals, especially during periods of high volatility.

Using these technical analysis indicators, you can decide which direction the trend is headed or if it is a consolidation. Do you feel bullish that the stock will rise? Are you Bearish, with an opinion the stock will be falling? You may feel the stock is trading in a range.

◆◆◆

When you place a trade for an option to get into the trade, you are placing an order to OPEN. If you sell an option contract to OPEN, your platform will list your trade order as STO (SELL to Open). Buying to open will be listed as BTO. To get out of a trade, you will CLOSE the position. If you sold the option to open, you will buy the option to close, BTC. If you buy to open, you will sell to close, STC.

OPEN	CLOSE
BTO	STC
STO	BTC

When you buy, you are in a long position. When you sell, you are short a position. In most cases, I prefer to sell to collect a premium. You can look at it like being an insurance company. You want to collect a premium with a high probability of being OTM. This way, the option expires worthless. You keep the premium and can sell another one.

Your account grows and gives you more buying power for future trades.

	BEARISH	BULLISH
BUY	Put	Call
SELL	Call	Put

The chart above is a reference to use if you are bullish or bearish. If you want to sell an option, you can see that you would sell a Call if you are bearish or a Put if you are bullish.

When you sell a Call or Put alone, this is called a naked position. A naked position you sell has limited profit with unlimited risk. A naked position you buy has unlimited profit, with the risk being the premium you paid. The naked position with unlimited risk is also called undefined risk.

PLACING THE TRADE

In this example, for Apple, you would go into the platform and pull up the ticker symbol AAPL. You open the options chain closest to 45 DTE. This would be the 46d. You have selected to sell a put at the 16 Δ. To do this, you click on the Bid price of 2.19. The order is set up at a 215 strike price for 2.33. The price of 2.33 is mid-price between the bid and ask price. You can see several fields with valuable information from the line under the options chain. A "POP" of 84% states that you have an 84% chance of making at least 1 cent on the option. "EXT" of 233 tells you there is $233 of extrinsic value. "P50" of 95% means there is a 95% chance the profit on the option will reach 50% sometime before expiration. "Max Profit" of 233 indicates the premium collected is 2.33 x 100. Max Loss is $ 21,267. If the stock goes to zero, you would be out by this amount. "BP Eff" is the buying power needed for this position. BPR (Buying Power Requirement) refers to the amount of capital a trader must have available to open and maintain a position. It represents the minimum funds or margin required by a broker to ensure the trader can cover potential losses from the trade. For options and margin accounts, brokers often calculate this based on the risk and leverage of the trade. The more expensive an option is, the higher the buying power required. If you are in a naked position, an increase in volatility (IV) will increase the buying power requirement since it increases the value of the option. This is an important consideration for not using all your buying power.

In most cases, once you have gotten into a trade, you will manage your position to avoid having a maximum loss. If you are concerned about the possible max loss or the buying power is too high, you can put on a defined risk trade. This is done by simply adding a "leg" to the position. Simply click on the "ask" price in the options chain on the line of the strike you choose for the "leg" further OTM. This turns the Naked Put into a Put Credit Spread. You'll learn about different strategies in Chapter eight.

In the AAPL (Apple) example, if you buy a put further OTM, your Max Loss is lower, and so is the buying power requirement. However, the premium collected is also reduced. You can move the long Put further OTM or closer, depending on if you are trying to collect more premium or reduce buying power. Moving the long Put further OTM will cause the buying power to increase as the premium credit will increase. When the order type says Net Credit, you are receiving a premium. In other words, you are selling to open the position. You can see the order in the left corner. You have STO for the Put you sell and BTO for the put you buy. Because the Put you sell costs more, you will collect a net credit.

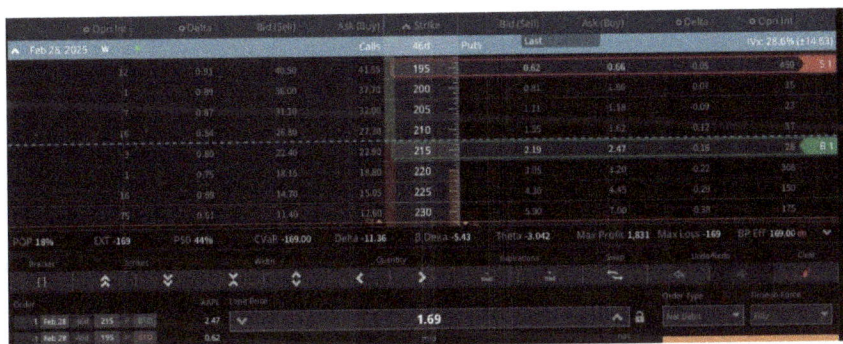

Opn Int	Delta	Bid (Sell)	Ask (Buy)	Strike	Bid (Sell)	Ask (Buy)	Delta	Opn Int
Feb 28 2025			Calls	46 d	Puts	Last		IVx 28.6% (±14.61)
12	0.93	40.50	41.65	195	0.62	0.66	-0.05	430	S 1
1	0.91	36.00	37.70	200	0.81	1.96	0.01	35
1	0.87	31.30	32.00	205	1.11	1.18	-0.09	23
16	0.84	26.90	27.30	210	1.35	1.42	0.17	57
1	0.80	22.40	22.92	215	2.19	2.47	-0.15	28	B 1
1	0.75	18.15	19.80	220	3.05	3.20	0.22	308
16	0.69	14.70	15.05	225	4.30	4.45	0.21	150
75	0.61	11.40	11.60	230	5.30	7.60	0.37	175

| POP 18% | EXT -169 | PSO 44% | CVaR -189.00 | Delta -11.36 | β.Delta -5.43 | Theta -3.042 | Max Profit 1,831 | Max Loss -169 | BP Eff 169.00 |

Order		AAPL					Order Type	Time in Force
1 Feb 28 215	2.47		1.69				Net Debit	Day
1 Feb 28 195	0.62							

Using the same AAPL example, if you swap the buy and sell, you now enter into a long position, known as a Put Debit Spread. You see how the max profit and max loss are opposite the short position in the previous example. You will pay a premium of $169 for this position. Because it is far OTM, as a long position, it would have a very low probability of profit—18% POP in this example.

Before you click to send an order for a trade, you can move the legs for your trade around to understand how the POP, Max Profit, Max Loss, and BP Eff are affected. Remember, you are not placing an order yet. You are just looking at different setups for potential trades. After a while, you'll learn how these movements impact the "bottom line" variables and it will become second nature. Some platforms have an analysis tab you can view before placing the trade, where you can see what changes in volatility, price, and time will do to the resulting profit or loss of the position.

When you place the order, you can set it as a market or limit order. If you choose a market order, you will typically not get a fill price as good as a limit order. But you will get a quicker fill. A limit order set at mid-price will tell the market maker to fill your order for no less than the price you selected on a sell order or no more than the price you selected on a buy order. When you put in the order as a limit order, and it doesn't fill for a while, you can adjust the price up or down to get a fill.

When you are placing the order, it defaults to DAY. In the example, on the right bottom side is the word DAY. Just above is the wording "Time-in-Force." Day means the order will remain in force until it fills or the end of the Day. If it is not filled by the end of the day, the order will be canceled. You can change the time-in-force to GTC. GTC is for "Good til Cancelled." This means the order will remain on until you cancel it unless it is filled.

After you have reviewed and feel ready to place the trade, you will click a "review & send" button. This will display a confirmation of the trade you set up with the buying power required and give you another chance for review. If it looks correct and you are ready to place the trade, you can click send. This will execute the trade.

Here is another trade example:

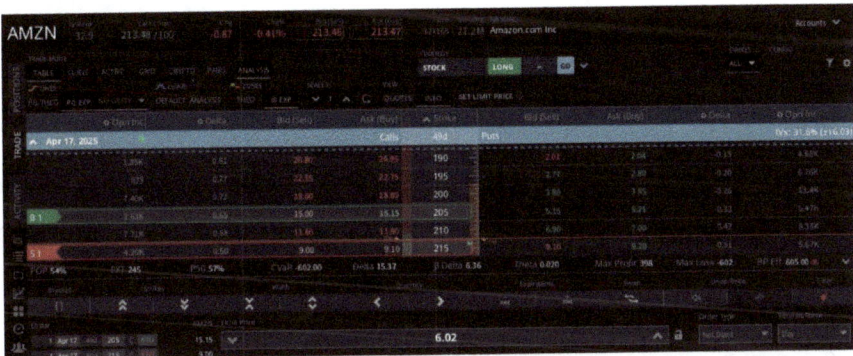

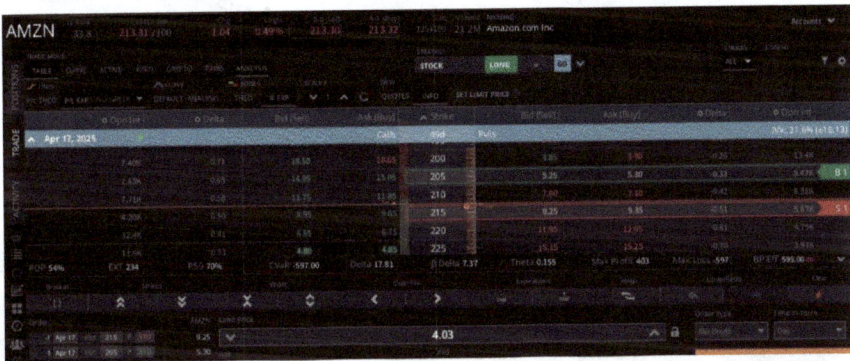

The above two images are trade setups for a 49 DTE spread. Both are bullish plays. You have a bullish assumption, expecting the price to rise in the next 49 days. The top image is a net debit. This is buying a call debit spread for $602 (6.02 x 100). The 2nd image is a net credit. This is selling a put credit spread for $403 (4.03 x 100). The breakeven is the same on both at ~210.94. When buying the call, you have more Extrinsic value, less Delta, and less Theta. Your P50, the probability of reaching 50% profit before expiration, is greater when selling the put spread.

Earlier in the chapter, there was a discussion on things to keep in mind in your selection. One thing is when you buy an option, the extrinsic value should not exceed one-third (33%) of the total option premium. In this case, the call debit spread has an extrinsic value of 245. This is 40% of the premium. You can move the long call further ITM, or move the short call further OTM to reduce the extrinsic value as shown in the following two images. Price was fluctuating and IV rank was increasing during the trade setup. This affects your entry as well.

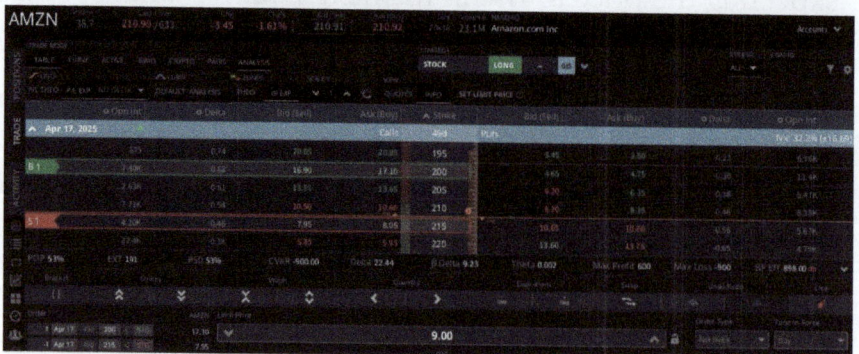

Once you have decided on the direction of the trade and the strikes to choose, you are ready to click REVIEW & SEND. When you place a trade, your platform will give you a breakdown of the trade for your review before you actually click send. Different strategies to use for trades will be discussed in detail in the chapter on mechanics of strategies.

If you are a beginning trader, it is strongly recommended for you to paper trade at first and always start out small until you get the hang of things. I was doing well and a bit too comfortable with myself in the beginning. By taking too much risk and not following the rules I caused my account to have a large drawdown (loss in balance). I felt like I was starting all over again. The key to avoiding the large drawdowns is managing risk and following your rules. Don't let emotion come into play. We will discuss managing risk next.

HOW DO YOU MANAGE RISK

A mistake made by some traders is trading too big. You will win most of your trades if you stay mechanical and follow the rules. Make no mistake, there will be losing trades. Nobody wins 100% of their trades. However, you don't want a loss to take months to make up. At most, you want to limit your loss to 200%-250% of the credit you received. For instance, if you receive $500 as credit, you don't want to risk losing more than $1000 if the trade is a loser. That way, it only takes a few trades to regain the loss. Be careful to watch how much buying power you use. You can think of "Buying Power" as the collateral you are required to have on hold in case the trade goes against you. If volatility expands, your undefined risk trades will have an increase in buying power requirements. You need to have room for this expansion. During the August 2024 volatility expansion, many people saw their buying power increase above 100%. This results in a need to close positions that could have recovered had the buying power been available. The volatility quickly contracted. These are called outlier losses. With a significant volatility expansion, it is generally for a short period and falls quickly. A good rule to follow for allowing volatility expansion is to allocate your buying power according to VIX. The lower the VIX, the higher the chance for a higher volatility expansion. Use less buying power with a lower VIX. In low VIX environments, long positions would work well. Your value of the option would increase with a volatility spike.

When the VIX expands suddenly, the larger the points it increases, the faster it contracts back to its normal average of approximately 18.

Buying Power Usage Guidelines	
VIX	Max Portfolio Allocation
0-15	25%
15-20	30%
20-30	35%
30-40	40%
40+	50%

In addition to the size of your buying power usage, you should use caution in the size of each trade. Using no more than 5% BPR (buying power requirement) per position is a good idea. You may need to go up to 7% with a smaller account. You don't want to put all your eggs in one basket. You need to diversify to limit losses. There are several ways to diversify.

Diversify in underlying.

If you have all of your positions in AAPL and AAPL has some negative news causing the stock to tank, you could incur significant losses by having too much invested in one underlying. When you are starting with a small account, under $25k, it may be difficult to diversify much. Once your account is large enough, try not to exceed 25% of buying power usage in any one underlying.

You want to choose to trade many non-correlated stocks. If two stocks are highly correlated, if one goes down, the other does as well. For example, take peanut butter and jelly. The demand for peanut butter is highly correlated with jelly. If there's a demand for peanut butter and jelly sandwiches, a decrease in demand will cause a reduction in peanut butter as well as jelly. This is a positive correlation. If they are negatively correlated, the rise of one would result in the fall of another. Noncorrelated would be like ice cream and banking. They have nothing to do with each other. If there were big news affecting banking and causing the bank stocks to fall, this would not affect ice cream. You can look at products in different asset classes, such as Oil vs Gold or stocks vs bonds. Different sectors can be used for diversification, such as tech, consumer discretionary, financial, industrials, energy, real estate, etc. It is also good to look at how the stock is correlated to the market as a whole, the S&P. How does the volatility of a stock move compared to the market?

Futures offer low correlation. The ticker for futures begins with "/." For instance, the S&P 500 futures, E-mini S&P, is /ES. Natural Gas is /NG. Here is a chart showing the correlation between the futures.

	/ES	/YM	/NQ	/RTY	/UB	/ZB	/NB	/NF	/NT	/GE	/SI	/GC	/CL	/NG	/ZC	/ZW	/ZS	/6E	/6B	/6J	/6C	/6A
/ES	1																					
/YM	0.81	1																				
/NQ	0.75	0.51	1																			
/RTY	0.65	0.55	0.45	1																		
/UB	-0.39	-0.46	-0.2	-0.51	1																	
/ZB	-0.39	-0.47	-0.19	-0.53	0.98	1																
/NB	0.4	-0.48	-0.2	-0.49	0.88	0.92	1															
/NF	-0.37	-0.46	-0.17	-0.44	0.81	0.88	0.97	1														
/NT	-0.33	-0.4	-0.18	-0.39	0.64	0.73	0.87	0.92	1													
/GE	-0.28	-0.44	-0.26	-0.25	0.48	0.5	0.55	0.55	0.55	1												
/SI	-0.25	-0.37	-0.23	-0.35	0.45	0.51	0.56	0.52	0.47	0.37	1											
/GC	-0.39	-0.49	-0.29	-0.46	0.62	0.66	0.72	0.67	0.59	0.47	0.86	1										
/CL	0.12	0.19	15	0.06	0.08	0.02	0	-0.04	-0.07	0.04	-0.15	0.01	1									
/NG	0.09	-0.04	0.09	-0.06	0.06	0.14	0.13	0.15	0.17	0.12	0.08	0.15	-0.02	1								
/ZC	-0.01	-0.01	0.03	-0.04	0.19	0.17	0.12	0.11	0.09	0.12	0.05	0.11	0.26	0.06	1							
/ZW	-0.04	-0.01	-0.06	0.15	-0.01	-0.02	-0.01	-0.04	-0.05	0.05	0.1	0.07	0.24	0	0.51	1						
/ZS	-0.12	-0.21	-0.03	-0.09	0.22	0.19	0.14	0.11	0.05	0.13	0.19	0.23	0.24	0.17	0.55	0.27	1					
/6E	-0.25	-0.21	-0.2	-0.28	0.35	0.34	0.4	38	0.35	0.29	0.29	0.47	-0.1	0.09	0.02	0	0.15	1				
/6B	-0.18	-0.25	-0.11	-0.07	0.21	0.19	0.19	0.2	0.11	0.31	0.27	0.4	0	-0.08	0.02	0.07	0.13	0.54	1			
/6J	-0.52	-0.56	-0.4	-0.52	0.76	0.75	0.81	0.75	0.68	0.58	0.54	0.71	0.03	0.03	0.15	-0.03	0.2	0.52	0.27	1		
/6C	-0.19	-0.2	-0.17	-0.16	0.22	0.24	0.34	0.31	0.26	0.15	0.38	0.41	0.07	0.05	0.13	0.07	0.33	0.44	0.28	0.37	1	
/6A	-0.24	-0.24	-0.24	0.2	0.48	0.48	0.51	0.46	0.37	0.36	0.48	0.57	-0.02	0.04	0.2	0.14	0.35	0.57	0.44	0.54	0.7	1

Looking at the correlation chart, /ES is negatively correlated with gold/GC. The correlation of /ES with the Euro, /6E, is negatively correlated at -.25. As /ES increases, /6E tends to fall slightly. The Russell (/RTY) is highly correlated with /ES at .65. As /ES rises, /RTY will also tend to move higher—just not a 1:1 movement. A correlation of 1 indicates an underlying will move in volatility at the same rate as the underlying in reference.

NOTE: Not all futures and not all stocks have options available. You can tell when you pull up the underlying on your brokerage platform, and no options chain is displayed.

Another way to examine how a stock moves in correlation with the market is to assess its beta. Beta measures the movement velocity of a stock relative to the S&P 500 or SPY. A stock with a beta above one moves with greater volatility than the S&P.

Diversify by strategy.

BPR expands with an increase in volatility for undefined risk trades. The BPR for defined risk trades is capped at the limited loss. For this reason, you should use defined risk trades along with your undefined risk trades.

Diversify by expiration.

By choosing different expirations, you allow for corrections in the market and corrections in the underlying. Looking at a candlestick chart of any underlying will show some periods of up and some periods of down. The stock will technically have a cycle. This can be seen as a stock reaches the top of a Keltner channel and pulls back to the mean, or 21 SMA. This is where a technical analysis with MACD or stochastic comes in handy. Although they are not leading indicators, they can give hints on where the stock is within the cycle.

HOW DO YOU PREPARE

The steps to prepare to place a trade are summarized as follows:

1. Check your available buying power.

2. Decide on the underlying to trade.

3. Choose an expiration date.

4. Decide on a defined or undefined risk strategy.

5. Make a directional assumption.

6. Decide your strikes.

While the steps to placing a trade are personal preference, this guide can help you make your decision manageable. Depending on the market conditions, you may change the order of the steps.

Check your available buying power.

The first step in putting on a trade is to check your buying power. As stated in Chapter 6, keeping your buying power usage percentage within the level based on the VIX is wise. If you only use defined risk strategies, you may use a higher BPR % without adding the additional risk of an increase in buying power requirement. When you buy options, the BPR is the cost of the premium you paid to open the position. When you sell an option, the BPR is like an escrow account where the amount of risk is placed on hold as protection from a possible loss. As you will learn in Chapter 8, when we discuss managing the trade, you must keep buying power available to make trade adjustments when needed.

Decide on the underlying to trade.

Do you want to trade options on a stock, ETF, or future? There are advantages to each. Stocks have earnings each quarter. They also have company and sector risks that cause changes in volatility. The change in volatility of stocks happens more often in stocks than in ETFs or futures. This can provide more opportunities for higher premiums. If you are going to trade options on a stock, you should check for the company earnings release date. This is the day, each quarter, a company announces its earnings and future predictions on profits or losses. Stocks can have volatile moves around earnings. It's good to try to avoid trading around earnings. There are some trades set up specifically for trading around earnings. I would recommend using earnings trades sparingly as they carry more risk. When you choose your underlying, a quick way to check for earnings release date is in the options chain.

The purple line in the image with "E" represents an earnings release date. It falls between the two option chains' expiration dates, with the release date shown. Futures and ETFs do not have earnings releases. The options chains with "W" are weekly expirations. The highlighted chains in each month are the monthly expirations.

Whether you trade a stock, EFT, or future, there are some criteria you should consider when choosing. A key factor in selecting the right underlying is liquidity. In trading options, you want to look at the liquidity of the options. An underlying with good liquidity should have a good selection of timeframes and strike prices. There should be good open interest as well as tight bid/ask spreads. It is probably not very liquid if you only see the monthly time frame for the 3rd Friday of every month. Most liquid stocks have monthly expiration as well as weekly expiration options available. Are the strike prices available by 5-point increments? Strike prices on the options chain can vary. Some will have strikes in increments of 1, such as 100, 101, 102, 103, etc. Some will be 5-point increments like 100, 105, 110, 115, etc. Some may have only 25-point increments, such as 100, 125, 150, 175, etc. Further out options chains on the SPX, such as a LEAP (option dated 1 year out) will have 25-point increments. However, the closer to expiration options are 5-point increments. A suitable liquid stock could be five strikes and, in some cases, 1.

An example of AMZN shows liquidity in the 44 DTE options with an expiration date of Feb 28. This is in the weekly expiration. The strikes to choose from are by five strikes. The column listing open interest shows many strikes, with over 100. Some stocks may not have good open interest in the weekly expirations but do in monthly expirations.

If you look at the difference between the Bid and Ask prices, referred to as the spread, a tight range is typically less than .20. In AMZN on the Feb 28 weekly expiration, the bid/ask spread is less than .20, signaling liquidity. You need liquidity to prevent having difficulty closing a position when it's time to get out of the trade. Liquidity is equally essential whether it's a stock, ETF, or future.

You want to sell options with high volatility for a higher premium. There are watchlists you can use to sort by IVR. You can make your own watchlist to include stocks you trade regularly. Since volatility does not stay elevated for long, you can also use the column of increased volatility over the past 5 days. This is a good starting point for picking your options. Here is an example of a personal watchlist I created, sorted by IVR. The last column is the 5-day change in IVR.

Symbol	Last	Chg	Chg%	⌄ IVR	IVx 5dCh
/ZSH5	1,035.50	16.50	1.62%	77.8	4.3%
/ZWH5	539.25	1.75	0.33%	52.8	19.9%
GLD	249.24	-1.35	-0.54%	51.7	-0.4%
COIN	295.48	13.85	4.92%	47.6	9.3%
PDD	105.57	5.31	5.30%	33.3	4.1%
XLI	137.73	0.80	0.58%	32.8	-3.5%
AMAT	192.05	5.57	2.99%	30.8	-2.5%

Choose an expiration date.

How long do you plan to be in the trade? The closer your trade is to expiration, the larger your P/L swing will be. Longer durations allow time to manage a trade if adjustments are needed. Longer durations cause your buying power to be in use longer and may result in a lower daily P/L. With buying power tied up, you have fewer occurrences to trade. This is where I agree with the use of the closest to 45 DTE options. You want to try to stay with expirations between 30 and 60 days. Shorter than 30 is hard to manage if the trade goes against you. Longer than 60 days can take longer to reach profit potential. You should spread out your trades to get a good variance on expiration dates. Therefore, your positions aren't all expiring on the same date. In other words, put a few trades on each week. Then, if you are using the closest to 45 DTE, you will have some expiring on the weekly expiration and some expiring on the monthly expiration. This gives you diversification by expiration date.

Decide on a defined or undefined risk strategy.

Defined risk strategies mean the maximum loss is capped, and it is known when the trade is placed. Defined risk trades have a lower BPR. In other words, less capital is required. They also come with lower P/L compared to undefined risk trades. A long options strategy is a form of a defined risk trade. The maximum loss is the premium paid to open the position. A short options strategy with a further out-of-the-money long trade offers protection against outlier losses. This is referred to as a spread. Undefined trades offer higher POP. Undefined risk trades can increase in BPR if volatility increases or the price moves closer to being ITM.

The mechanics of individual strategies will be described in detail in chapter eight. While there are dozens of different strategies out there, they are all simply a combination of Calls and Puts. I will introduce two common strategies here. A "Strangle" is an undefined strategy involving a short "naked" Call and a short "naked" Put. The Call or Put by itself is considered "naked" because it is traded alone with no wing for protection. This is a position you will place when you don't expect the price of an underlying to move much. You have an assumption that it is in consolidation and trading within a range. You turn an undefined risk trade into a defined risk trade by buying "wings". This is where you buy a Call or Put further out of the money. There will be more details in the next chapter. Here is a chart of the most common strategies for selling options, listing as defined or undefined risk and a directional assumption listed:

DIRECTIONAL ASSUMPTION	DEFINED UNDEFINED	STRATEGY	MECHANICS
Bullish	undefined	Naked put	short OTM put
Bearish	undefined	Naked Call	short OTM call
Bullish	defined	Put credit spread	short OTM put, long put further OTM
Bearish	defined	Call credit spread	short OTM call, long call further OTM
Neutral	undefined	Strangle	short OTM put, short OTM call
Neutral	defined	Iron Condor	put credit spread with a call credit spread

*Two ways to think of an Iron Condor. 1) A Put Credit Spread on the Put side and a Call Credit Spread on the Call side. 2) a short strangle with a long strangle further OTM for "wings."

The advantage of using a strangle as a trade over a naked call or a naked put is that you are collecting premium for both the Call side and Put side, playing for a neutral position with little movement in price. The disadvantage with a strangle or a naked option is that, as an undefined strategy and depending on the price and IV of the option you are trading, as well as your account size, the BPR may be too much. This is where adding the wings in the Iron Condor will help reduce BPR. Adding a wing, the long Put or Call, to a naked option to make it a Put Credit Spread or a Call Credit Spread will also limit the BPR.

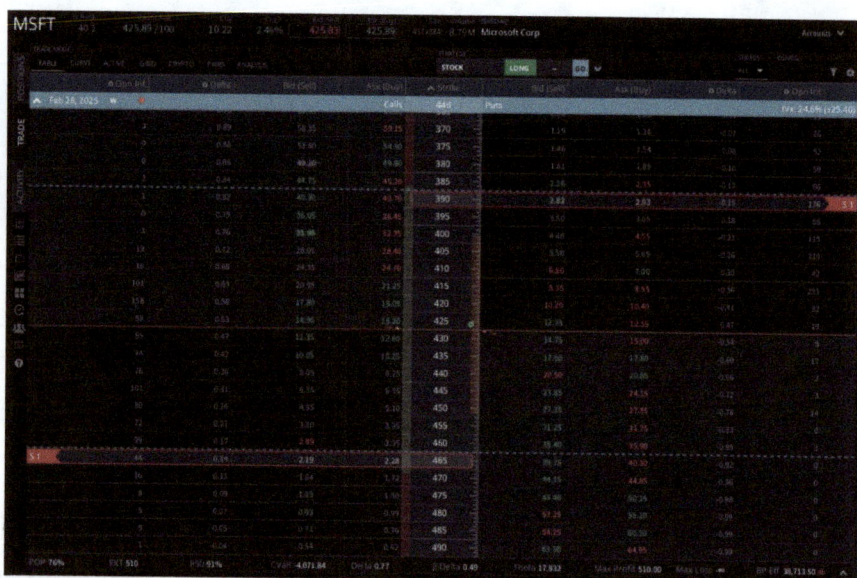

A 16Δ strangle in MSFT. When there is no 16Δ available, you choose the next nearest Δ. Selling a call around 16Δ and selling a put around 16Δ creates the strangle. A few things to note in this example: the 16Δ is right at 1σ, shown with the dotted line. The brown ruler extending from about the 401

strike to about the 451 strike is the expected move with the current IV. The green shading up and down is the profit zone to give you a visual of the breakeven point. The data line at the bottom shows that this strategy has a 76% POP. You'll collect $510 in premium, which is the EXT amount. This is the extrinsic value as well as the maximum profit. The BPR to put this trade on is $38,713.50. For a small to mid-sized account, this requires too much BPR. This is where you add the long wings in the following image.

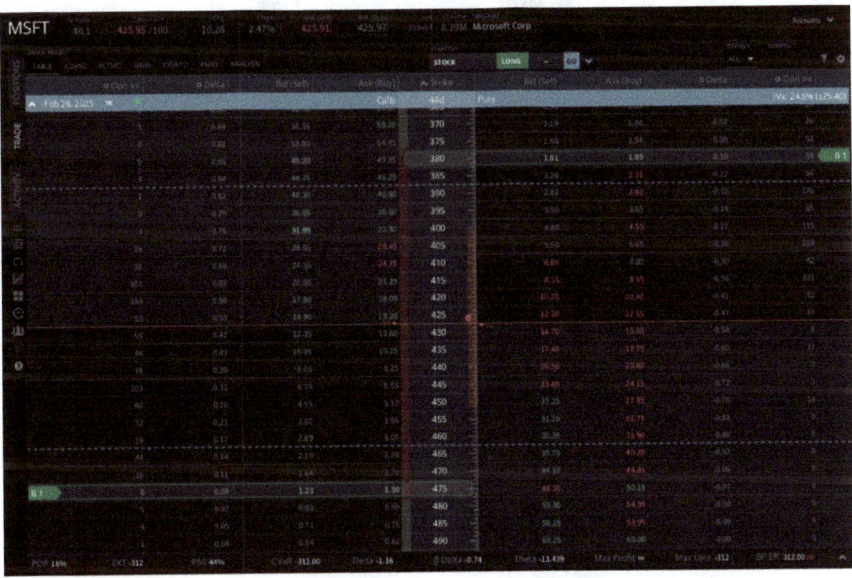

The price of long wings at ~10Δ are $312.

Each strike chosen for your trade is a leg in the position. When the long and short legs are added together, you have an Iron Condor. This reduces the premium received from $510 to $199 in the example, but it also reduces the BPR to only $800.

*If the BPR is available, you can move your "wings" further OTM to increase your profitability.

Here is a comparison of the ~16Δ strangle vs the 16Δ iron condor with 10Δ wings.

MECHANICS	16Δ STRANGLE	16Δ IRON CONDOR USING 10Δ WINGS
Long Call	---	-127
Short Call	223	223
Short Put	287	287
Long Put	---	-185
Net Credit	$510	$199
Max Loss	∞	1000-199=801
BPR	$38,716.50	$800

Max loss in a defined risk strategy is calculated using the max strike width between either the Call side or the Put side. In the MSFT example, the distance is equal on both the call and put side, at 10. The Formula is:

100 x "max strike width" – "Premium received"

100 x 10 – 199 = 801 max loss (also the BPR)

Make a directional assumption.

Do you feel the stock you are trading is in an uptrend or downtrend? Is it trading in a range? This is a directional assumption. What direction do you feel the stock is moving? This is where some of the technical analysis can be used. A directional assumption around IV can guide your decision to be bullish, bearish, or neutral. If the underlying you are looking to trade is surging to the upside, you take on less risk using a bullish trade instead of a neutral trade. Also, if the underlying is tanking to the downside and you assume it will continue, you should use a bearish trade. Also, look at the market trend as a whole, the S&P 500.

Decide your strikes.

You've gone through the steps to choose what you want to trade on, what duration, and a directional assumption. Now, it's time to pick your strike or strikes, depending on the strategy you are going with. There are three things to consider when making your strike selection. Remember in the discussion about the Greeks? Delta is how much an option price will move in correlation with the price of the underlying. An option with a delta of .10 will change by .10 for every dollar move in the stock price. Another way to consider delta is the probability the option will expire ITM. A 25Δ Put will have a 25% chance of expiring ITM. It also gives a 75% POP. If you use a 16Δ strangle, with a 16Δ Put and a 16Δ call, there is a 32% chance of one of the sides expiring ITM. This is in line with having a 68% POP. If a stock has skew, choosing the strike by delta will result in the put or call being further from ATM than the other. Skew in Calls or Puts results from the market fearing a more significant extreme move to one side. A trade entered with higher deltas will have higher swings in P/L throughout the duration of the trade. A higher delta will also come with a lower POP and higher BPR. Higher deltas come with higher profit potential. Lower deltas have lower premiums collected. Yet, the POP and theta are higher, which can result in profits being obtained sooner.

THE MECHANICS OF TRADE STRATEGIES

Part of being a successful options trader is choosing the right strategies. The number of strategies may seem overwhelming at first. A good way to start is to begin your trading with the most basic strategies until you get comfortable. I thought I could never learn all the strategies when I started to trade. The more you trade, the more it will come naturally. In this chapter, I will review many more popular trades. I will list whether the trade is suited for a bearish, bullish, or neutral outlook on the stock. The trade mechanics will be listed for how to construct the trade as well as profit and risk potential. All strategies are made up of combinations of Calls and Puts.

Here is a recap of the definition of Calls and Puts:

Call option: right to buy shares of a stock at the strike price when the stock is trading at a higher price in the market.

Put option: right to sell shares of a stock at the strike price when the stock is trading at a lower price in the market.

If you are bullish on a stock, you expect the stock price to rise between now and the option expiration date. You would use bullish strategies. You are bearish if you expect the stock price to fall. You would use bearish strategies. If you feel there is support and resistance demonstrating a range, you are neutral on the trend of the stock, not expecting much movement up or down, and would use a neutral strategy.

I recommend you start with these basic strategies:

- Naked Call

- Naked Put

- Call credit spread or Call debit spread

- Put credit spread or Put debit spread

- Strangle

- Iron condor

Each trade strategy is set up with a listing of steps in the position for ease of understanding. These trades are opened as one trade for each position. For example, an Iron Condor is to sell a Put credit spread and sell a Call credit spread. All four legs of the position are put on in one trade. The visuals also help to get you started with the proper setup of the trade and understand how it will profit.

COMMON BASIC BULLISH STRATEGIES:

You will want to use a bullish strategy when you have an assumption that the underlying you are trading is in an uptrend. I recommend you start with these basic strategies if you are bullish on the trade you want to place. These basic strategies involve a call and/or a put.

- Short Naked Put

- Put credit spread

- Long Naked Call

- Call debit spread

DIRECTIONAL ASSUMPTION	Neutral to Bullish
MAX PROFIT	Credit received
MAX LOSS	Short Put Strike x 100 - credit received
PROFIT TARGET	50% max profit
BREAKEVEN	Put strike - credit received
OPTIMAL	Stock rises and volatility falls
NOT OPTIMAL	Stock falls
MANAGE LOSING TRADE	Roll the short put out for a credit.
ITM at expiry	Will be assigned 100 shares if ITM at expiry. Close at a loss or roll out before expiration to avoid assignment.
OTM at expiry	Put expires worthless. You keep credit for max profit.

Sell an OTM put.

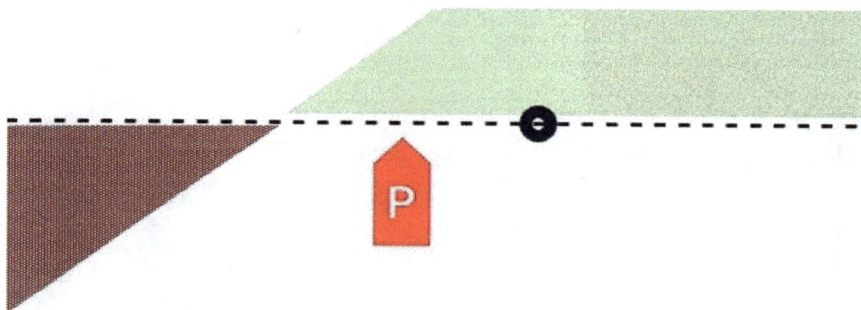

• Naked Puts will be profitable even if the stock falls some, as long as it stays above the strike price at expiration.

Put Credit Spread (short put spread)   defined risk

DIRECTIONAL ASSUMPTION	Neutral to Bullish
MAX PROFIT	Credit received
MAX LOSS	Width of the strikes - credit received
PROFIT TARGET	50% max profit
BREAKEVEN	Short put strike - credit received

OPTIMAL	Stock rises and volatility falls
NOT OPTIMAL	Stock falls
MANAGE LOSING TRADE	Roll the position out for a credit.
ITM at expiry	Close before expiration to avoid exercise. If partially ITM you will be assigned on the short put.
OTM at expiry	You keep credit collected for max profit.

Sell a put ATM or OTM. Buy a further OTM put.

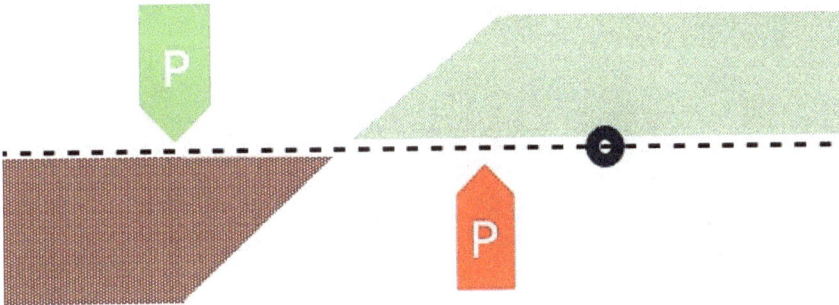

*Also referred to as a "Bull Put Spread."

DIRECTIONAL ASSUMPTION	Bullish
MAX PROFIT	unlimited
MAX LOSS	Debit paid for position
PROFIT TARGET	50% of debit paid
BREAKEVEN	Long call strike + debit paid
OPTIMAL	Stock price moves up
NOT OPTIMAL	Stock price falls
MANAGE LOSING TRADE	Generally, no management because you will pay more to roll the position.
ITM at expiry	Close the position before expiration to avoid losing time decay.
OTM at expiry	Max loss is realized.

Buy an ITM call.

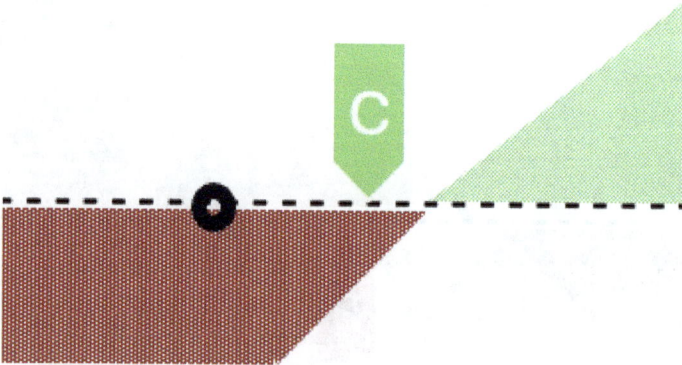

• Naked calls will have a higher chance of profit if purchased in the money. You need to have the underlying to increase in price in order to profit.

Call Debit Spread

DIRECTIONAL ASSUMPTION	Bullish
MAX PROFIT	Strike distance - debit paid
MAX LOSS	Debit paid for position
PROFIT TARGET	50% of max profit
BREAKEVEN	Long call strike + debit paid

OPTIMAL	Stock price moves up
NOT OPTIMAL	Stock price falls
MANAGE LOSING TRADE	Roll down the short call. Do not go past breakeven.
ITM at expiry	Max profit is realized.
OTM at expiry	Max loss is realized.

Buy an ITM call. Sell an OTM or ATM call.

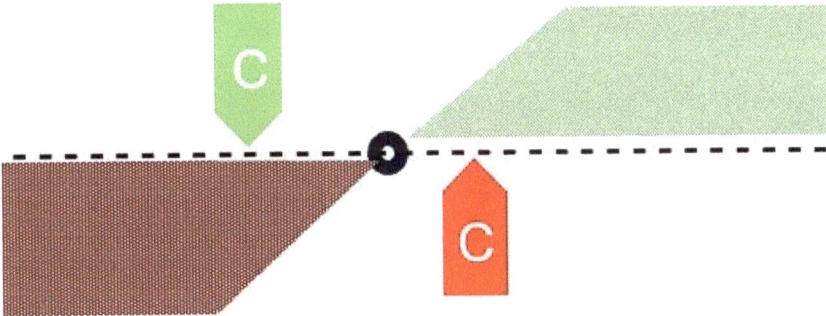

COMMON BASIC BEARISH STRATEGIES:

You will want to use a bearish strategy when you have an assumption that the underlying you are trading is in a downtrend. I recommend you start with these basic strategies if you are bearish on the trade you want to place. These basic strategies involve a call and/or a put.

- Short Naked Call

- Call credit spread

- Long Naked Put

- Put debit spread

Short Naked Call

DIRECTIONAL ASSUMPTION	Neutral - Bearish
MAX PROFIT	Credit received
MAX LOSS	unlimited
PROFIT TARGET	50% of max profit
BREAKEVEN	call strike + credit received
OPTIMAL	Stock falls
NOT OPTIMAL	Stock rises
MANAGE LOSING TRADE	Roll out in time for a credit.
ITM at expiry	Close before expiry to avoid assignment of short shares
OTM at expiry	Max profit

Sell a call OTM.

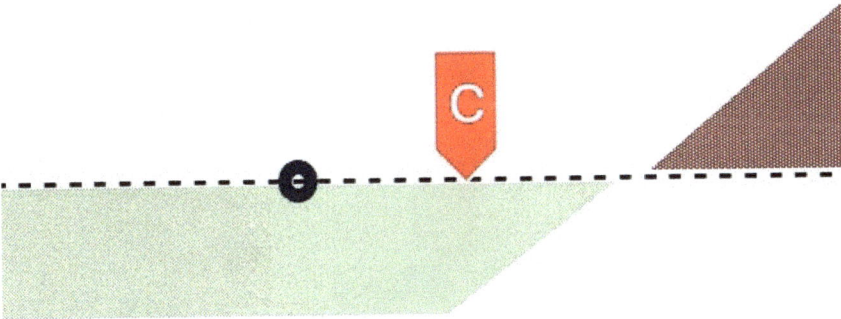

Call credit spread

defined risk

DIRECTIONAL ASSUMPTION	Neutral - Bearish	
MAX PROFIT	Credit received	
MAX LOSS	Width of strikes - credit received	
PROFIT TARGET	50% of max profit	
BREAKEVEN	Call strike + credit received	
OPTIMAL	Stock falls	
NOT OPTIMAL	Stock rises	
MANAGE LOSING TRADE	Roll out in time for a credit.	
ITM at expiry	Close before expiry to avoid assignment of short shares	
OTM at expiry	Max profit	

Sell an ATM or OTM call. Buy a further OTM call.

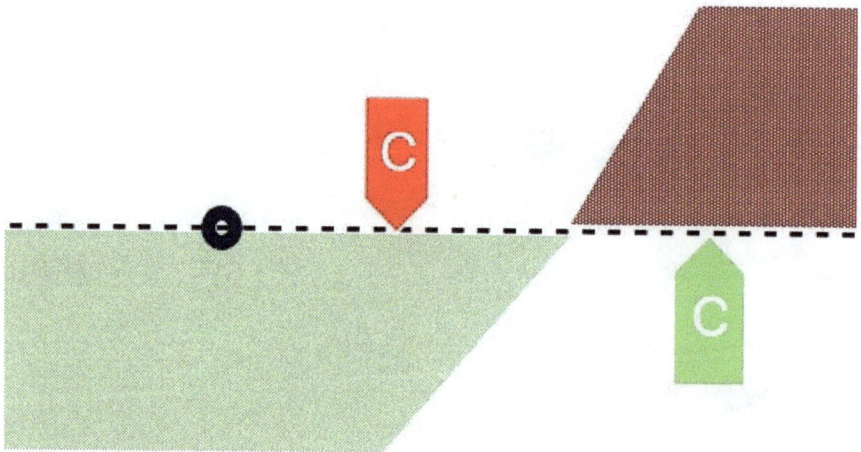

Long Naked Put

DIRECTIONAL ASSUMPTION	Bullish
MAX PROFIT	unlimited
MAX LOSS	Debit paid for position
PROFIT TARGET	50% of debit paid
BREAKEVEN	Long put strike + debit paid
OPTIMAL	Stock price moves down
NOT OPTIMAL	Stock price rises
MANAGE LOSING TRADE	Generally, no management because you will pay more to roll the position.
ITM at expiry	Close the position before expiration to avoid losing time decay.
OTM at expiry	Max loss is realized.

Buy an ITM put.

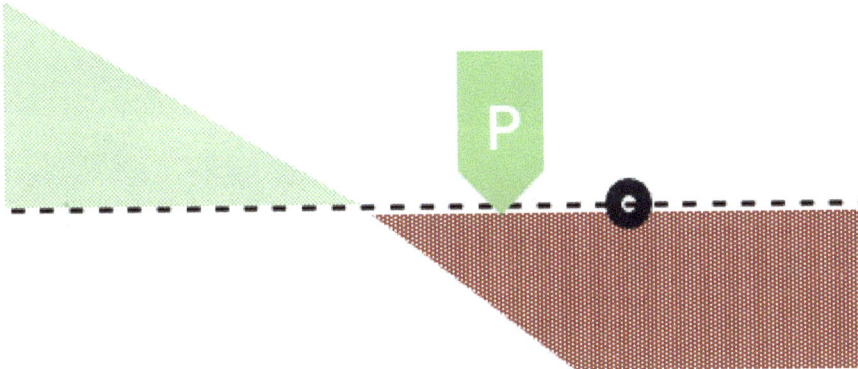

- Naked puts will have a higher chance of profit if purchased in the money. You need to have the underlying to decrease in price to profit.

Put Debit Spread

DIRECTIONAL ASSUMPTION	Bearish
MAX PROFIT	Width of the strikes - debit paid
MAX LOSS	debit paid
PROFIT TARGET	50% max profit
BREAKEVEN	Long put strike - debit paid
OPTIMAL	Stock falls
NOT OPTIMAL	Stock rises
MANAGE LOSING TRADE	Roll the short put closer to the long put for a credit staying below breakeven
ITM at expiry	Max profit
OTM at expiry	If partially ITM, close before expiry at loss to avoid exercise of long put

Sell an OTM put. Buy a put closer to ATM or buy a put ITM. This makes the long put cost more than the short put, resulting in a debit paid.

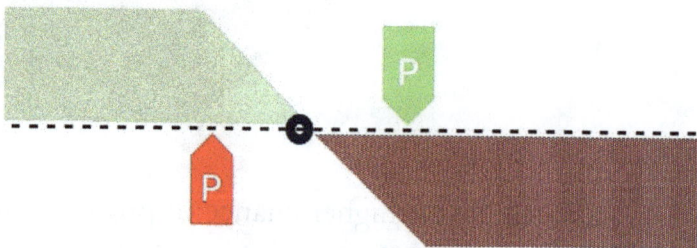

COMMON BASIC NEUTRAL STRATEGIES:

You will want to use a neutral strategy when you have an assumption that the underlying you are trading is in a consolidation. This means it is trading in a range without any large moves to the upside or downside. Neutral strategies will need the stock to stay close to the price when the trade was put on, or stay within range at expiration in order to profit. These usually take longer to reach profit than the other strategies. The strategies involve a Call and/or a Put.

- Strangle

- Iron condor

DIRECTIONAL ASSUMPTION	Neutral
MAX PROFIT	Credit received
MAX LOSS	Unlimited
PROFIT TARGET	50% of max profit
BREAKEVEN	Put strike - credit received Call strike + credit received
OPTIMAL	Stock stays between strikes
NOT OPTIMAL	Stock rises above call or falls below put
MANAGE LOSING TRADE	Roll the untested side closer to the tested side or roll both sides out in time
ITM at expiry	Roll out in time or close for loss
OTM at expiry	Max profit

Sell an OTM put and an OTM call.

DIRECTIONAL ASSUMPTION	Neutral
MAX PROFIT	Credit received
MAX LOSS	Width of the spread - credit received
PROFIT TARGET	50% of max profit
BREAKEVEN	Short put strike - credit received Short call strike + credit received
OPTIMAL	Stock stays between short strikes
NOT OPTIMAL	Stock rises above call spread or falls below put spread
MANAGE LOSING TRADE	Roll the untested side closer to the tested side or roll both sides out in time
ITM at expiry	Close for loss to avoid assignment
OTM at expiry	Close for max profit

Sell an OTM Put credit spread and sell an OTM Call credit spread.

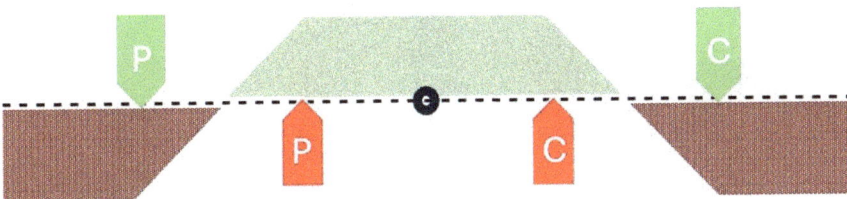

ADVANCED STRATEGIES:

Once you have mastered the basic strategies and want to try placing more advanced trades, I have included a few more advanced trades you can try.

- Covered Call

- Poor Man's Covered Call

- Call Zebra

- Call Butterfly

- Big Lizard

- Jade Lizard

- Covered Put

- Poor Man's Covered Put

- Put ZEBRA

- Put Butterfly

- Reverse Big Lizard

- Reverse Jade Lizard

- Short Straddle

- Iron Fly

- Call Broken Wing Butterfly

- Put Broken Wing Butterfly

BULLISH STRATEGIES

Covered Call

undefined risk

DIRECTIONAL ASSUMPTION	Bullish
MAX PROFIT	Short call - Purchase price of your shares of stock + Premium received
MAX LOSS	Stock purchase price - credit received
PROFIT TARGET	50% of Max Profit
BREAKEVEN	Stock purchase price - credit received
OPTIMAL	The stock price is ATM at expiration. Max extrinsic value is collected.
NOT OPTIMAL	The stock price falls. Your shares decrease in value. Your call will lose value. You will however keep the premium collected on the call.
MANAGE LOSING TRADE	You can roll it out in time, increasing extrinsic value. You can also move the call strike down in the same cycle. Avoid rolling the call below your breakeven.
ITM at expiry	The short call will be exercised, and your 100 shares will be "called away".
OTM at expiry	The short call expires worthless. You can deploy another.

This is a bullish stock position. This trade involves owning stock. You must own 100 shares of a stock. You sell an ATM or OTM call against your 100 shares. This reduces the cost basis of your shares. The risk for the call is "covered" by the 100 shares of long stock you own. No additional buying power is needed.

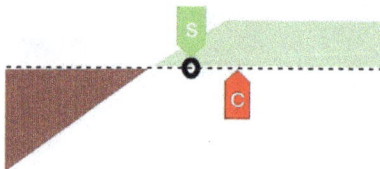

- To avoid losing your shares, you can roll the short call out in time and up a few strikes for a small credit before the call moves ITM.

DIRECTIONAL ASSUMPTION	Bullish
MAX PROFIT	Strike distance - debit paid + extrinsic value of long option
MAX LOSS	Debit paid for position
PROFIT TARGET	50% of Max Profit
BREAKEVEN	Long call strike + debit paid
OPTIMAL	The stock price is ATM at expiration. Max extrinsic value is collected.
NOT OPTIMAL	The stock price falls. Your shares decrease in value. Your call will lose value. You will however keep the premium collected on the call.
MANAGE LOSING TRADE	You can roll it out in time, increasing extrinsic value. You can also move the call strike down in the same cycle. Avoid rolling the call below your breakeven.
ITM at expiry	The short call will be exercised, and your 100 shares will be "called away".
OTM at expiry	The short call expires worthless. You can deploy another.

Sell a call OTM. In a further out expiration, buy a call ITM.

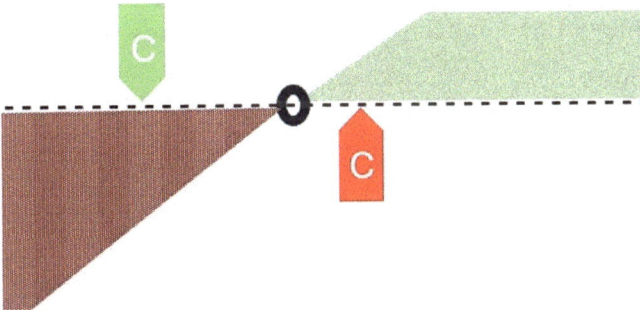

- Ensure the debit paid to enter the position does not exceed 75% of the width of the strikes.

	DIRECTIONAL ASSUMPTION	Bullish
	MAX PROFIT	unlimited
	MAX LOSS	Debit paid for position
	PROFIT TARGET	25% of Debit paid doe position
	BREAKEVEN	Short call strike + extrinsic value paid
OPTIMAL	Stock price moves up	
NOT OPTIMAL	Stock price falls	
MANAGE LOSING TRADE	Roll down the short call	
ITM at expiry	Close and reload in later expiration. Close before expiry to avoid assignment.	
OTM at expiry	Max loss is realized.	

Buy 2 ITM calls. Sell 1 ATM call. You want to remove all extrinsic value in the trade. This is an excellent stock replacement for an IRA account. The movement of the stock and the profit/loss in the position move 1:1. For every dollar the stock rises, your position adds $1 profit.

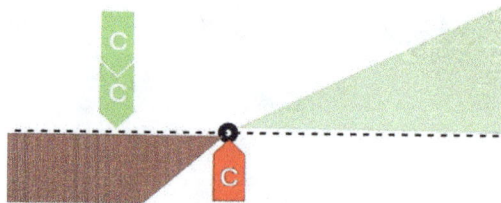

- The idea with the ZEBRA, which stands for zero extrinsic value, is to try to get your short call at .50 Δ and the two long calls at .70 Δ.

DIRECTIONAL ASSUMPTION	Bullish
MAX PROFIT	Width of long spread - debit paid
MAX LOSS	Debit paid for position
PROFIT TARGET	25% of long spread width
BREAKEVEN	Long call strike + debit paid

OPTIMAL	Stock remains between the 2 long call strikes.
NOT OPTIMAL	Stock is completely ITM or completely OTM.
MANAGE LOSING TRADE	Close the long spread when it is completely ITM. You may add Put credit spread to turn into an iron condor.
ITM at expiry	when partially ITM, profit is made. Close position before expiration. If completely ITM, close for loss before expiration to avoid assignment.
OTM at expiry	Close for a loss to avoid assignment before expiration.

Buy a Call ATM or just OTM. Sell two Calls further OTM. Buy a Call even further OTM the same distance from the short Calls as the other long Call. This makes the wings (long Calls) equal distance from the body (2 short Calls).

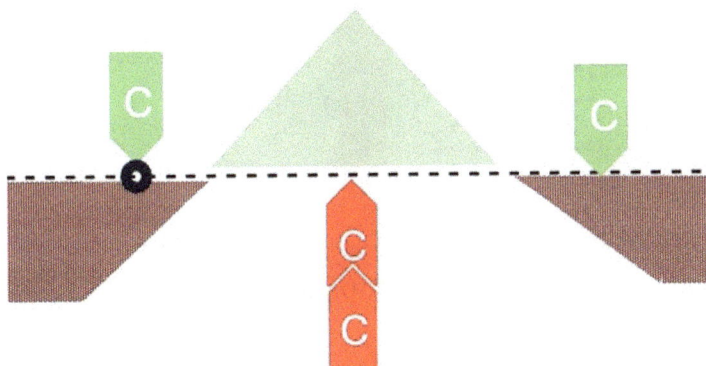

DIRECTIONAL ASSUMPTION	Bullish
MAX PROFIT	Credit received
MAX LOSS	Short Put Strike x 100 - credit received
PROFIT TARGET	25% max profit
BREAKEVEN	Short put strike - credit received

OPTIMAL	Stock stays within breakeven range staying close the short put.
NOT OPTIMAL	The stock falls below breakeven
MANAGE LOSING TRADE	Roll the short put down and out if it is still ITM near expiration. Close the short call spread or put another call spread against the
ITM at expiry	when partially ITM, profit is made. Close position before expiration. If completely ITM, close for loss before expiration to avoid assignment.
OTM at expiry	Close for a loss to avoid assignment before expiration.

Sell a call spread with the short call ATM. Sell a put ATM.

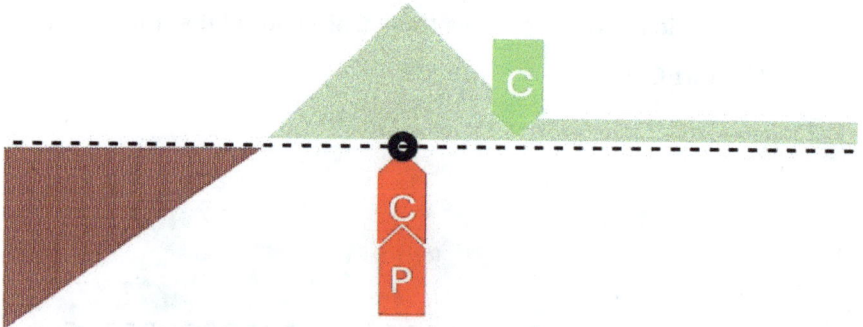

- Credit received needs to be greater than the width of the call spread to eliminate upside risk.

DIRECTIONAL ASSUMPTION	Neutral to Bullish
MAX PROFIT	Credit received
MAX LOSS	Short put strike x 100 - credit received
PROFIT TARGET	50% max profit
BREAKEVEN	Short put strike - credit received

OPTIMAL	Stock stays between short strikes
NOT OPTIMAL	Stock falls below short put strike
MANAGE LOSING TRADE	Roll the short put out to a further expiration for a credit, turning it into a naked put. You can also roll down the call credit spread
ITM at expiry	Close before expiration to avoid exercise.
OTM at expiry	You keep credit for max profit.

Sell an OTM put. Sell an OTM call credit spread.

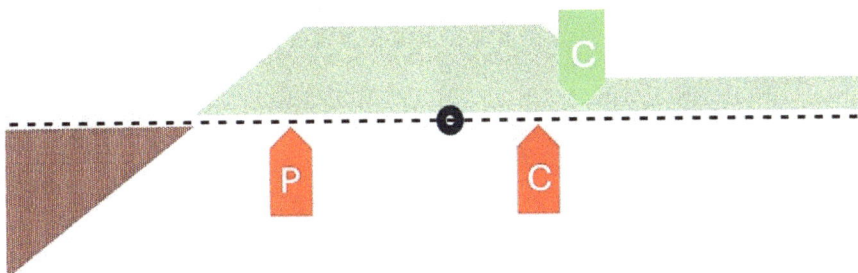

- There is no risk to the upside if the credit you receive is greater than the width of the call credit spread.

BEARISH STRATEGIES

Covered Put

undefined risk

DIRECTIONAL ASSUMPTION	Bearish	
MAX PROFIT	Difference between price of shorted stock & short put + credit received	
MAX LOSS	unlimited	
PROFIT TARGET	50% max profit	
BREAKEVEN	Short stock price + credit received	
OPTIMAL	Stock moves down	
NOT OPTIMAL	Stock rises	
MANAGE LOSING TRADE	Roll the put out for a credit or roll the put up in current duration staying below breakeven	
ITM at expiry	Put will be exercised against 100 short shares of stock. Max profit realized	
OTM at expiry	Put expires worthless. You keep the credit received. You are still short 100 shares and can set up another covered put position.	

Short 100 shares of stock. Sell an ATM or OTM put.

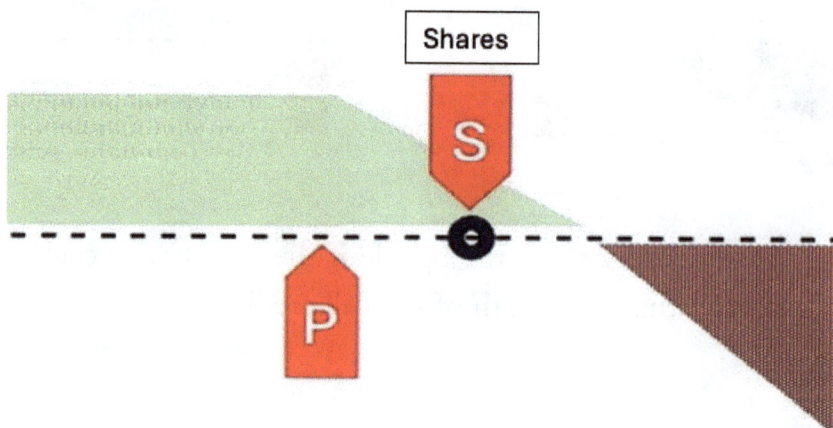

DIRECTIONAL ASSUMPTION	Bearish
MAX PROFIT	Width of the strikes - debit paid + extrinsic value in long option
MAX LOSS	debit paid
PROFIT TARGET	50% max profit
BREAKEVEN	Long put strike - debit paid
OPTIMAL	Stock falls to the short put
NOT OPTIMAL	Stock rises
MANAGE LOSING TRADE	Roll the short put out in time or move the short put up in current expiry. staying below breakeven
ITM at expiry	Max profit
OTM at expiry	Max loss

Buy an ITM put. Sell an OTM put at a closer expiration.

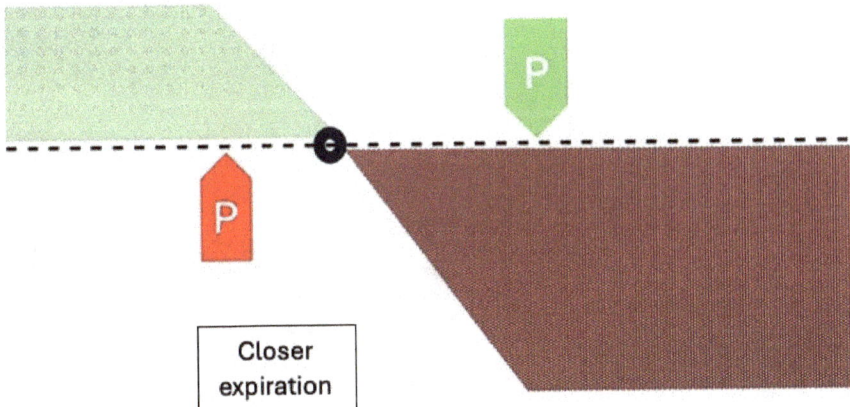

Closer expiration

DIRECTIONAL ASSUMPTION	Bearish
MAX PROFIT	unlimited
MAX LOSS	debit paid
PROFIT TARGET	25% of debit paid
BREAKEVEN	short put strike - extrinsic value paid
OPTIMAL	Stock falls
NOT OPTIMAL	Stock rises
MANAGE LOSING TRADE	Roll the put up in the same expiration
ITM at expiry	Close for profit. If partially ITM close for loss to avoid assignment
OTM at expiry	Max loss

Sell a put ATM. Buy 2 ATM puts to remove all extrinsic value.

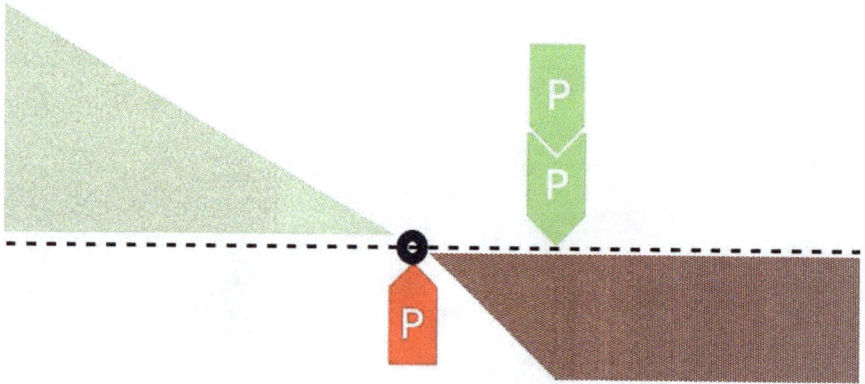

- This makes a great short stock replacement for IRA account.

Put Butterfly   defined risk

DIRECTIONAL ASSUMPTION	Bearish
MAX PROFIT	Width of long spread - debit paid
MAX LOSS	debit paid
PROFIT TARGET	25% of long spread width
BREAKEVEN	Long put strike - debit paid

OPTIMAL	Stock stays between long strikes
NOT OPTIMAL	Stock rises or falls further than one of the long strikes
MANAGE LOSING TRADE	Can manipulate the trade into an iron condor or close the long spread if it is near full value and leave the credit spread on.
ITM at expiry	Close at loss before expiration to avoid assignment in fully ITM. If partially ITM, will have a profit. Take profits
OTM at expiry	Close at loss before expiration to avoid assignment

Buy and ATM or OTM put. Sell 2 puts further OTM. Buy a put even further OTM keeping the same distance from the short puts as the first long put. This makes the wings the same width. Think of it as a put credit spread and a put debit spread with the short puts having the same strike.

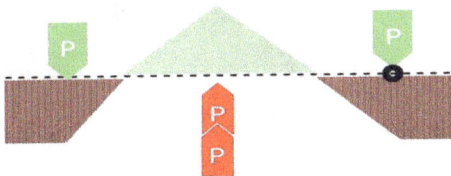

- This is a low probability trade. Another way to trade this strategy is if you are confident about a sell off you can position the trade around the expected move.

Reverse Big Lizard   undefined risk

DIRECTIONAL ASSUMPTION	Bearish
MAX PROFIT	Credit received
MAX LOSS	unlimited
PROFIT TARGET	25% of max profit
BREAKEVEN	Short call strike - credit received

OPTIMAL	Stock stays between breakeven range
NOT OPTIMAL	Stork rises or falls further than one of the long strikes
MANAGE LOSING TRADE	Roll the position out in time
ITM at expiry	Take profits and close before expiration to avoid possible assignment.
OTM at expiry	Position is always ITM

Sell an ATM call. Sell and ATM put credit spread with the same short strike as the ATM call.

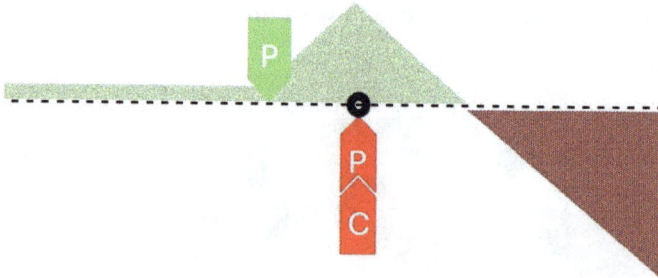

- This position has no downside risk. Make sure the credit received exceeds the width of the put spread.

Reverse Jade Lizard

DIRECTIONAL ASSUMPTION	Neutral - Bearish
MAX PROFIT	Credit received
MAX LOSS	Unlimited
PROFIT TARGET	50% of max profit
BREAKEVEN	Short call strike + credit received
OPTIMAL	Stock stays within range
NOT OPTIMAL	Stock rises above breakeven
MANAGE LOSING TRADE	Roll short call out in time or roll up the put spread
ITM at expiry	Close before expiry to avoid assignment of short shares if ITM on call side
OTM at expiry	Max profit

Sell an OTM put credit spread. Sell an OTM call.

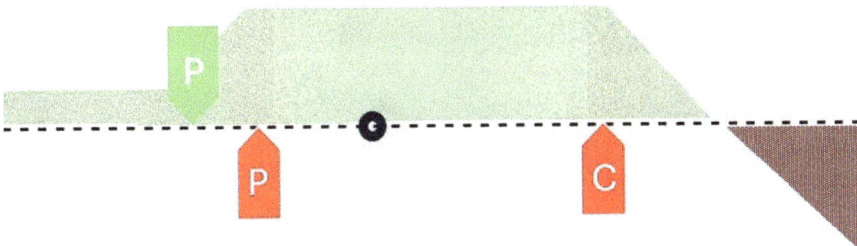

Short Straddle   undefined risk

DIRECTIONAL ASSUMPTION	Neutral
MAX PROFIT	Credit received
MAX LOSS	Unlimited
PROFIT TARGET	25% of max profit
BREAKEVEN	Put strike - credit received Call strike + credit received

OPTIMAL	Stock stays between breakeven points
NOT OPTIMAL	Stock rises above call or falls below put
MANAGE LOSING TRADE	Roll the untested side closer to the tested side or roll both sides out in time
ITM at expiry	Must close before expiration
OTM at expiry	Always ITM.

Sell an ATM call and an ATM put.

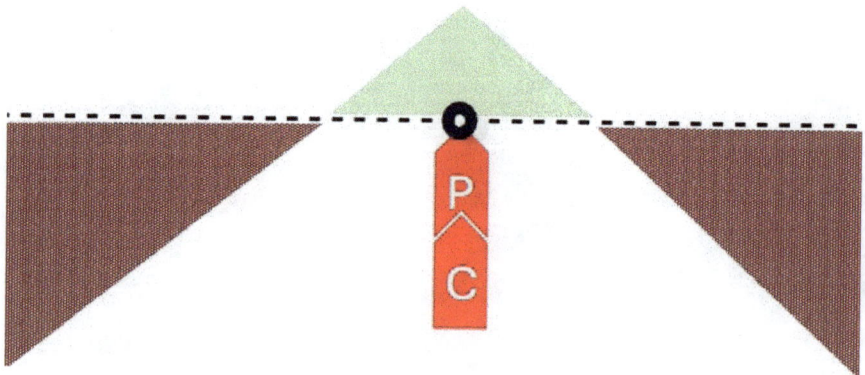

Iron Fly   defined risk

DIRECTIONAL ASSUMPTION	Neutral
MAX PROFIT	Credit received
MAX LOSS	Widest spread - credit received
PROFIT TARGET	25% of max profit
BREAKEVEN	Short put strike - credit received Short call strike + credit received
OPTIMAL	Stock stays between breakeven points
NOT OPTIMAL	Stock rises outside of breakeven points
MANAGE LOSING TRADE	If not completely ITM, you can roll the untested long put to tighten the wing if able to do for a credit.
ITM at expiry	Close for loss to avoid assignment
OTM at expiry	Close for max profit. One side will always be at least partially ITM

Sell an OTM put spread with the short put ATM. Sell an OTM call spread with the short call ATM.

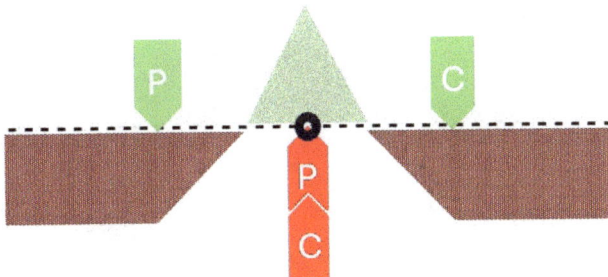

- Similar to a call butterfly or put butterfly. But it uses calls and puts together. It is done for a credit.

DIRECTIONAL ASSUMPTION	Omnidirectional
MAX PROFIT	Width of long spread + credit received
MAX LOSS	Short spread - long spread - credit received
PROFIT TARGET	50% of credit received
BREAKEVEN	Short call strike + (long spread width + credit received)
OPTIMAL	Stock stays below breakeven point
NOT OPTIMAL	Stock rises above position for entire position to be ITM
MANAGE LOSING TRADE	can restructure to an iron condor
ITM at expiry	Close for loss to avoid assignment
OTM at expiry	Expires worthless. Keep credit for profit

Buy a long call strangle. Sell 2 calls closer to the ATM call. This creates a butterfly with uneven wings.

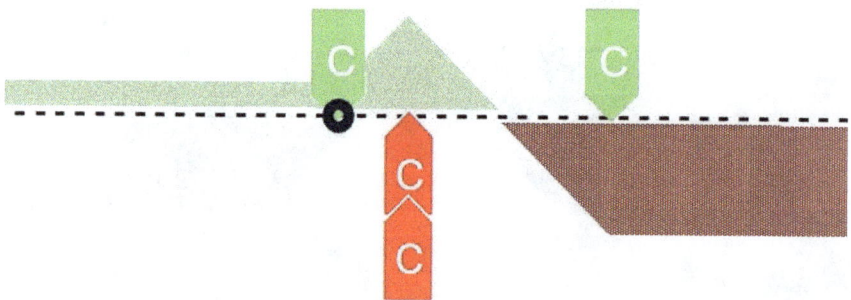

- Call Broken Wing Butterfly is a good strategy on a stock with call skew.

Put Broken Wing Butterfly

DIRECTIONAL ASSUMPTION	Omnidirectional	
MAX PROFIT	Width of long spread + credit received	
MAX LOSS	Short spread - long spread - credit received	
PROFIT TARGET	50% of credit received	
BREAKEVEN	Short call strike + (long spread width + credit received)	
OPTIMAL	Stock stays above breakeven point	
NOT OPTIMAL	Stock falls below position for entire position to be ITM	
MANAGE LOSING TRADE	can restructure to an iron condor	
ITM at expiry	Close for loss to avoid assignment	
OTM at expiry	Expires worthless. Keep credit for profit	

Buy a long put strangle. Sell 2 puts closer to the ATM call. This creates a butterfly with uneven wings.

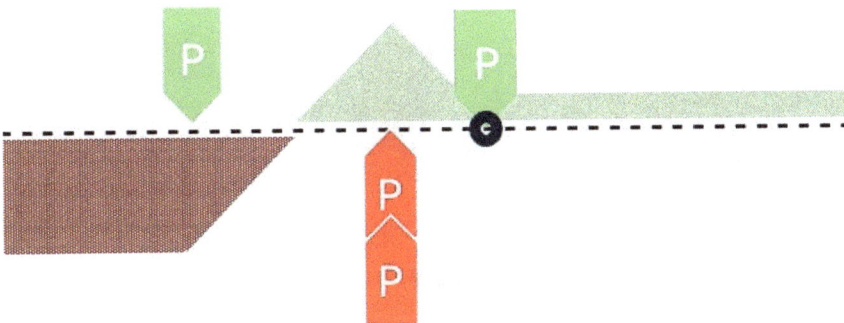

- Put Broken Wing Butterfly is a good strategy when the stock has put skew.

MANAGING YOUR TRADES

Managing trades in a portfolio is crucial for several reasons, as it directly impacts the investment strategy's performance, risk, and overall health. In portfolio management, trades are the mechanisms that adjust the portfolio's composition to reflect your goals, market conditions, and risk tolerance. Properly managing these trades ensures the portfolio aligns with your objectives and performs optimally over time.

Here are the key reasons why it's essential to manage trades in a portfolio:

Risk Management

Balancing risk: Every trade you make changes your portfolio's risk profile. For example, buying a volatile stock or option can increase risk, while selling an asset can reduce it. Without active management, your portfolio may become too risky or too conservative.

Diversification: Trades help maintain diversification. If your portfolio becomes too concentrated in a particular asset class, sector, or stock, you may expose yourself to higher risks. Active management of trades ensures that the portfolio maintains its diversification across different assets and reduces unsystematic (individual) risks.

Managing Correlation: Managing trades ensures that the portfolio's assets don't have high correlations with each other. If assets move in the same direction simultaneously, the portfolio's risk becomes more concentrated. Regularly managing trades helps maintain low correlations between assets, thus reducing overall portfolio risk.

Adapting to Market Conditions

Dynamic environment: Markets constantly change, and economic, political, and social conditions can impact asset prices. For example, certain stocks may become more volatile during a market downturn, while others (e.g., bonds, gold) may become safer havens.

Rebalancing for new conditions: Managing trades allows you to rebalance your portfolio to adapt to these changes. For instance, if you hold an overweight position in equities and the market is becoming more volatile, you should reduce your exposure to equities and increase your allocation to safer assets like bonds or defensive stocks.

Market cycles: Different market cycles (e.g., bull and bear markets) require different portfolio strategies. Active management allows tactical shifts to align with market cycles, such as rotating sectors or adjusting the overall exposure to equities vs. fixed-income assets.

Capitalizing on Opportunities

Exploiting inefficiencies: By actively managing trades, you can capitalize on perceived market inefficiencies or mispriced assets. For instance, if you identify an undervalued stock, you can buy an option on it with the expectation that its price will rise over time.

Tactical decisions: Short-term opportunities, such as earnings beats, geopolitical events, or technical patterns, may warrant changes in your portfolio. Active trade management allows you to take advantage of these opportunities, increasing the potential return of the portfolio.

New information: As new information becomes available (e.g., company earnings reports, macroeconomic data, interest rate decisions), active management allows you to adjust the portfolio in response to this data quickly.

Achieving Financial Goals

Aligning with objectives: Portfolio management is driven by your specific financial goals, whether you want to grow wealth, generate income, or preserve capital. Managing trades allows you to adjust the portfolio to align with these goals consistently.

Time horizon management: Your investment goals may be short-term (e.g., saving for a vacation or a down payment on a house) or long-term (e.g., retirement, financial freedom). Managing trades ensures that your portfolio is structured appropriately for the time horizon, adjusting risk and asset allocation as you approach milestones.

Ensuring liquidity: Regular management of trades ensures that you can access the cash when needed. For example, suppose you need liquidity for a specific financial event. In that case, you may need to close positions to generate cash for buying power without negatively affecting the portfolio's long-term objectives.

Optimizing Tax Efficiency

Tax-loss harvesting: Active management of trades can help optimize tax efficiency. If a position in the portfolio is losing, you can close it to realize a tax-deductible loss (known as tax-loss harvesting). This can offset taxable gains from other positions and reduce the overall tax liability.

Capital gains management: Section 1256 of the Internal Revenue Code (IRC) is a provision in U.S. tax law that specifically deals with the taxation of certain types of financial instruments, including futures contracts, foreign currency contracts, section 1256 options, and regulated futures contracts. This section provides special tax treatment for these financial instruments, allowing for more favorable capital gains tax treatment.

60/40 Tax Treatment:

60% of gains or losses are treated as long-term capital gains (subject to long-term capital gains tax rates, which are typically lower than ordinary income tax rates).

40% of gains or losses are treated as short-term capital gains, which are taxed at the ordinary income tax rates.

This split is beneficial for taxpayers because the long-term capital gains tax rate is generally lower than the short-term rate. Even if the contract is held for less than a year, the tax treatment of the gains is still divided into this 60/40 split.

Instruments Covered by Section 1256: Section 1256 applies to a wide range of financial instruments and options on these, including:

• Futures contracts (e.g., commodity futures, stock index futures)

- Foreign currency contracts

- Non-equity options (such as broad-based index options)

Performance Optimization

Maximizing returns: Actively managing trades allows you to fine-tune the portfolio for optimal performance. For example, if one strategy or stock is outperforming others, you can reallocate capital to take advantage of that outperformance. Conversely, if a strategy or stock underperforms or doesn't meet your expectations, you can close positions to avoid further losses.

Rebalancing: Over time, the performance of different assets in your portfolio can shift your desired allocation. For instance, if stock options have done well and now represent a more significant portion of the portfolio than intended, you may close positions and invest in underperforming asset classes (like bonds or international equities) to return the portfolio to its target allocation.

Managing Volatility

Reducing drawdowns: Actively managing trades can help reduce significant losses (drawdowns) during periods of market volatility. For example, using stop-loss orders, hedging strategies, or diversifying into more stable assets (like bonds or defensive stocks) can reduce the risk of significant negative swings in the portfolio value.

Smoothing returns: Adjusting asset allocation based on changing market conditions can smooth the portfolio's returns and reduce the impact of short-term volatility. This is particularly important for risk-averse investors sensitive to large fluctuations in portfolio value.

Steps to use for reviewing each of your individual trades to determine if any action is needed:

- Are any trades at 50% or above profit?

- Are any trades at or near 200% loss?

- Are any trades at 21DTE (midpoint)?

- Is anything out of line? Is the price stretched above 2 ATRs?

You have profitable trades.

The first step in reviewing your trades is to take off your winners and lock in your profits. Look to see if any trades are at 50% profit or more. If there are, close the position and take your profits. This frees up buying power and gives you capital to reallocate. Some strategies take longer to reach 50% profit and benefit from you taking profits at 25%. This applies if you have any butterfly trades. In addition, consider daily profit. If a trade has gone your way quickly, it is beneficial to take profits early and redeploy capital. The rule is to look at what 50% profit would be. Let's say you have a trade on where you collected $200. 50% profit would be $100. On a 45-DTE trade, you would generally exit the trade at 21 DTE. In other words, you would be in the trade for 24 days. If at 50% profit, that would equate to 4.17 per day. If you exceed the daily P/L quickly, the average will decrease the longer you stay in the position. For example, reaching 25% in 5 days, that's $10 per day in profit. Take the profits and reload. This is shown in the following table.

	profit	Average duration	daily P/L
50% profit	100	24	4.17
25 % current profit	50	5	10

You have losing positions.

Look at the profit % on losing trades. Determining the risk depends on whether you are doing a defined risk or an undefined risk strategy. For defined risk, you would use the BPR. For undefined risk, you would use the premium credit times 2. Defined risk trades have the loss capped based on the width of the spread for a short position or the premium paid in a long position. As undefined risk trades become a losing position if the price goes in the wrong direction, the position could turn around. However, once it is at a 200% to 250% loss, the chances of it turning around drastically decrease. This is where you should exit the trade at a loss to stop the bleeding on the trade. Before closing this losing trade, check to see if it is possible to roll out to a further expiration and collect a credit. When you "roll" a position, you are closing the trade and opening the same strike in a further-out expiration. Sometimes, you can roll the strike up or down as needed. The "roll" keeps the dream alive and possibly turns the loss into a win.

Pull up the curve view on a losing trade. Does it look like there is a chance to still become profitable? Here is a chart of a put credit spread on /SI. It is a directional trade. Because of this, it is losing at the moment. The price moved closer to the strike since putting on the trade. However, today's price action is moving up, as you can tell by the .079 "Chg" on the top line. The brown area on the chart is the expected move. The position is still out of the expected move. There's plenty of hope for this trade to turn into a winner.

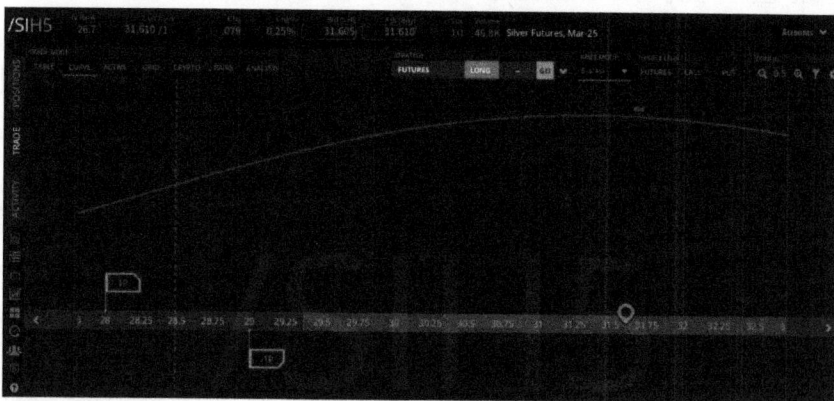

Another way to review losing trades is to look at the PoP (Probability of Profit). On the positions tab, you can set a column to list PoP. This will change as the delta of the position will change.

The /SI example shows that the PoP is 81%. If there is still time before 21 DTE, anything over 70% is worth leaving on longer.

Look for trades nearing 21 DTE.

Another way to check your trades is to look at the column labeled DTE. Is the trade at 21 DTE? If you put on a position shorter than 45 days, is it at the midpoint? For example, a 10 DTE trade at 5 DTE. This is the time to decide if the position is profitable. If so, close the trade and lock in the profit. Is the position losing? Check the PoP and look at the chart to decide if you feel it will win closer to expiration or if you should roll the position.

If you stay mechanical and follow the rules, you will win most of your trades. Don't let emotion take over. You can also perform technical analysis, looking at the chart of the stock to determine how the price is acting and whether you need to recenter any positions.

Your Assumptions Have Changed

Look at the chart for each position. Do the moving averages indicate a change in trend? When the 13 EMA and 34 EMA are crossing, you have a signal for a change in trend. On some stocks, you may use the 8 EMA and 21 EMA. Where is the price in regard to the Keltner channels? Looking at what price has done in the past, is it near 2 or 3 ATRs and indicating a pullback coming? This may signal a time to get out of the trade. You can take profits or roll the position out in time.

Managing trades in a portfolio is critical to achieving optimal performance, controlling risk, and aligning with an investor's financial goals. Through thoughtful and strategic management of trades, an investor can adapt to market conditions, capitalize on opportunities, minimize risk, and ensure the long-term sustainability of their investments. It also helps optimize tax efficiency, reduce volatility, and align the portfolio with the investor's risk tolerance and investment philosophy. A portfolio can become misaligned with the investor's goals without proper trade management, leading to suboptimal performance and higher risk.

MANAGING YOUR PORTFOLIO

The goal of portfolio management is to review your portfolio to keep your account in alignment with your financial objective, risk tolerance, and time horizon. You seek to achieve financial goals such as retirement savings, education funding, home purchasing, or generating income. In addition, you look to achieve financial freedom. You must maximize return and minimize risk for your portfolio to achieve your goals. You need to monitor your portfolio to ensure your portfolio continues to align with your goals and market conditions. You must determine If or when trades should be added or closed and what types of trades should be made.

Things to consider in managing your portfolio:

- Total buying power.

- % buying power used per underlying.

- Deltas and Thetas.

Manage total buying power usage.

The first step is to manage trades according to the previous chapter, Managing Your Trades. This way, you can free up buying power before examining the portfolio as a whole. If you have used up too much buying power, consider closing some profitable positions to release some buying power.

Your buying power usage should stay in the range according to the VIX, as you learned in Chapter six, with 25% to 50% usage. You can go up to 75% BPR if you primarily use defined risk trades. Options allow for high leverage, meaning a relatively small investment can control a significant position. If you're not managing your buying power carefully, you could over-leverage yourself, meaning you may have too many positions open or too much exposure to risk relative to your capital. This can lead to significant losses if the market moves against you.

Properly managing your buying power means you will always have available capital to enter new trades as opportunities arise. If you're too tied up in existing positions, you may miss out on potentially profitable trades because you don't have the capital to open new positions.

You might take on excessive risk exposure if you're overly focused on using your available buying power. This can leave you vulnerable if the market moves unexpectedly. By managing your buying power, you can keep a buffer to handle unexpected market volatility without closing positions prematurely.

Keep in mind that you need to have BPR available in case there is a need to roll a trade when managing your trades. For instance, if you have an Iron Condor that needs to be rolled further out in time, you need to have enough buying power to roll one side at a time. If your Iron Condor has 10 wide strikes for the wings, it uses $1,000 of initial buying power (not including the credit from the premium). There are four legs to roll the Iron Condor. You can only place a trade with four lines. Two legs will be closed and two reopened in the new position during a roll. You can only move two legs at a time. This causes an additional $1000 BPR in the middle of the roll when you have only rolled one side. This makes it two separate trades until the other side is rolled. The BPR goes back down when the other side is rolled.

Manage Buying Power Usage per Underlying.

Some traders make the mistake of putting too many eggs in one basket. You should not have over 30% of your total portfolio in any one stock. This is more difficult with an account under $25K. You can visualize the buying power allocation like a heatmap.

Here is an example of an ideal account that uses options on futures and has a small stock holding. The allocation of buying power is diversified by underlying.

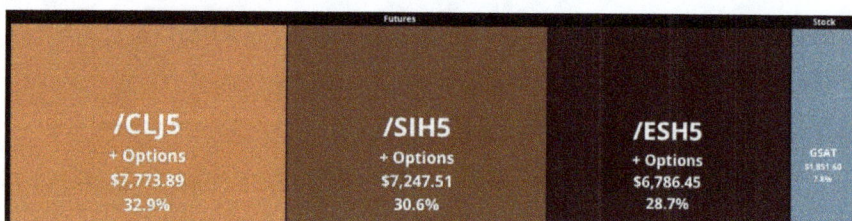

Futures			Stock
/CLJ5	/SIH5	/ESH5	GSAT
+ Options	+ Options	+ Options	$1,851.60
$7,773.89	$7,247.51	$6,786.45	7.8%
32.9%	30.6%	28.7%	

Managing buying power in options trading is about balancing risk and opportunity. It ensures you don't over-extend yourself with leverage, protects you from margin calls, helps you maintain flexibility to take advantage of new trades, and allows you to manage your portfolio effectively. By carefully monitoring your buying power, you can trade with a greater sense of security, avoid unnecessary losses, and position yourself for long-term success. Properly managing your buying power is essential to sound risk management and a disciplined trading approach.

Manage your Greeks.

The goal of your portfolio is growth without too much risk. Look at the deltas and thetas in your portfolio. Based on the current market environment, you should be as close to delta-neutral as possible and have as much theta as possible for income generation.

- Delta: Max of 0.2% of Account Net Liq (Net Liquidating Value)

- Theta: Minimum of 0.4% of Net Liq

Net Liquidating Value, referred to as Net Liq is the total value of all assets in a trading account if everything were sold and all liabilities were paid off at that moment. It includes cash, current market value of positions, and subtracts any margin or loan balances. It reflects the real-time worth of your account.

Adjusting for high or low deltas in an options portfolio is crucial for managing the risk and maintaining the desired exposure to the underlying asset. The delta of an option measures how much the option's price will change for a $1 move in the underlying asset. A high delta means the option behaves more like the underlying asset, while a low delta means it is more likely to act like a less sensitive or more speculative instrument.

Here are the key strategies to consider in adjusting for high or low deltas in an options portfolio:

Adjust for High Delta (Close to 1 or -1):

High delta options (like deep in-the-money Calls or Puts) move very closely with the price of the underlying asset. If you have a portfolio with a high delta and want to reduce the exposure to the underlying asset, you can:

Hedge with Opposite Positions

Sell high delta options: If you have long positions in high delta calls or puts, you can sell them (or roll them) to options with a lower delta.

Buy opposite position (to balance): If you are long a high delta Call, you can buy a high delta Put to neutralize the directional risk.

Use Spreads

Vertical spreads: If you have long Calls or Puts with high deltas, you could implement vertical spreads (buying and selling Calls or Puts at different strike prices but with the same expiration). This limits the overall delta of the position while still maintaining some directional exposure.

Use Other Strategies to Neutralize Delta

Straddles/Strangles: These strategies, involving buying a Call and a Put, can give you a more balanced exposure to both upside and downside moves, potentially lowering the overall delta.

Delta Neutral Strategies

Delta neutral trades involve setting up positions where the combined delta of all options is near zero. For instance, you can combine long and short options (in different expirations or strikes) to offset the high delta of your position.

Adjust for Low Delta (Close to 0):

Low delta options (like far out-of-the-money Calls or Puts) are less sensitive to the price movements of the underlying asset. These options are often used for speculative purposes or when traders anticipate significant price moves.

Increase Delta with More Sensitive Options

Buy options with higher deltas: If you want to increase the delta of your portfolio, you can buy options with higher deltas (such as closer-to-the-money options or options with shorter expirations).

Roll into higher delta options: If you have low delta options that are far out-of-the-money, consider rolling them to a higher delta (closer-to-the-money) strike price.

Use Spreads to Increase Delta

Vertical spreads: Similar to reducing high delta, you can also use vertical spreads to increase delta by selecting a strike that's closer to the current price of the underlying asset.

Ratio spreads: This strategy involves buying a certain number of options and selling a higher number of options, which could increase the delta exposure depending on the strikes selected.

Adjust Expirations

Shorter-term options: Shorter expiration options tend to have a higher delta closer to expiration, particularly for at-the-money options. Moving into a shorter-term expiration can increase the delta of your position.

Longer-term options: If you need less delta, you might choose longer-term options (long-dated options often have a lower delta because the time value dampens sensitivity to price movements).

Use Delta to Adjust Overall Portfolio Exposure:

In a delta-neutral strategy, the overall delta of your portfolio is close to zero. This means that small price movements in the underlying asset won't significantly affect the overall value of your options. This can be achieved by balancing long and short options with complementary deltas or using combinations of options and the underlying asset (e.g., stock). You can rebalance your portfolio by regularly checking the weighted delta of your entire options portfolio (if you have multiple positions) and rebalance it to maintain your desired level of exposure.

Monitor and Adjust as the Market Moves

Since deltas are dynamic (they change with the price of the underlying asset, the time to expiration, and changes in volatility), regularly monitor your portfolio and make adjustments based on how the market is moving. In addition to delta, consider the other Greeks (gamma, theta, vega, etc.) as they can provide insight into how your options positions will behave as market conditions change.

Consider this example:

Imagine you hold a portfolio of options with a total delta of +100, meaning it behaves like owning 100 shares of the underlying asset. If the stock moves by $1, your portfolio will move by $100 in value.

To reduce delta: You could sell options or use strategies like vertical spreads (selling Calls or Puts) with lower delta. Alternatively, you could buy Puts (if long) or Calls (if short) to hedge against significant moves in the underlying.

To increase delta: You could buy additional Calls or Puts with higher deltas or roll existing positions into more sensitive strikes or expirations.

THETA

You want some positive theta working for you when you sell options.

VIX	Max Theta
< 15	0.001 (.10%)
15 - 20	0.002 (.20%)
20 - 30	0.003 (.30%)
30 - 40	0.004 (.40%)
> 40	0.005 (.50%)

First, look at your deltas on your portfolio. Are they exceeding .2 % of net liq? A good delta/theta ratio to use is .5. For 100 Theta, you would carry a Delta of 50.

Adjusting for high or low theta in an options portfolio is crucial for managing the time decay (the erosion of an option's price as it approaches expiration). Theta represents the rate of change in an option's price due to the passage of time, with all other factors held constant. Positive theta means the position will benefit from time decay (generally seen in options that are sold). In contrast, negative theta means the position loses value as time passes (typically associated with long options positions).

Here's how you can adjust for high or low theta in an options portfolio:

Adjust for High Theta (Short Positions or Sold Options)

If your portfolio has high theta, it means you're selling options, or you're in positions where time decay is working in your favor. This typically occurs with strategies like Short Calls, Short Puts, Credit Spreads, or other strategies where you're selling options.

Hedge or Reduce High Theta Exposure

Buy Long Options (with negative theta): If you want to offset high theta, consider buying options (which have negative theta) to balance out your portfolio. For instance, if you have many Short Calls or Puts, buying long options can reduce the overall negative impact of theta decay.

Roll Positions: You can roll your short options positions (e.g., Short Calls or Puts) into later expiration dates. This will reduce the immediate impact of time decay, as options further from expiration have lower theta. However, this action may increase your exposure to other factors, such as volatility or risk.

Convert to Calendar or Diagonal Spreads: These strategies involve buying longer-dated options and selling shorter-dated options at the same or different strike prices. The long option (which typically has lower theta) mitigates the impact of time decay from the short option.

Example: You could sell a near-the-money short-term Call (high theta) and buy a long-term out-of-the-money Call (lower theta). This would reduce the portfolio's net theta, especially if the longer-term Call decays more slowly.

Shift to More Neutral or Less Aggressive Strategies

Iron Condors:

If you're selling options with high theta (such as in a short Iron Condor), consider taking a less aggressive approach with your strikes or expiration dates. Reducing the width between the sold strikes or moving further from the money can lower your theta exposure.

Covered Calls: If you're heavily exposed to Short Calls, rolling into a Covered Call strategy where you own the underlying stock can also help mitigate risk by giving you a more stable position. Owning the stock helps buffer against any volatility or moves that affect your Short Calls.

Reduce Position Size

Decrease the Quantity of Short Options: If your portfolio's theta is very high, it may be a sign that you're taking on too much risk by selling options. You can reduce your exposure by decreasing the size of your short options positions.

Adjust for Low Theta (Long Positions or Purchased Options)

If your portfolio has low theta, you're holding long options (like long Calls or Puts) or other positions that lose value due to time decay. In this case, you should either reduce the negative effect of theta or find ways to increase theta in your portfolio.

Increase Theta Exposure

Sell Short-Term Options: If you want to take advantage of time decay, you can sell options with shorter expiration dates. Short-term options experience higher theta than longer-term options, so selling them would benefit you from quicker time decay.

Example: If you own long Calls or Puts with far-dated expirations, you might sell short-term options (like selling short-term Calls or Puts) to generate positive theta.

Implement **Credit Spreads**: A more favorable theta profile can be provided when you sell an option and buy another option at a different strike price. The short leg provides theta decay, while the long leg limits risk if the market moves unexpectedly.

Iron Condors and Butterflies: Iron Condors and Butterflies can be particularly effective for generating income from time decay, as they typically have a higher theta when the market is range-bound.

Use Calendar and Diagonal Spreads

These are more advanced options strategies to become familiar with. I've listed them here for knowledge if you need to use them to adjust your thetas.

Calendar Spreads: A Calendar Spread (buying a longer-dated option and selling a shorter-dated option at the same strike) has a positive theta profile, as the short option decays faster than the long option. By using Calendar Spreads, you can convert some of your long positions' negative theta into positive theta from the short position.

Diagonal Spreads: These are similar to Calendar Spreads, but you use different strike prices for the long and short options. This strategy can allow you to adjust the risk and reward based on the time decay of the short option.

Close or Reduce Long Option Positions

Exit Long Options: If you are long options with very low theta (i.e., options far out-of-the-money or long-dated options), the negative impact of theta will erode the value of your position over time. Consider selling some of your long options to reduce exposure to theta decay.

Sell Half of Your Long Positions: If you have a significant long options position, selling half of it will reduce the negative theta exposure while still allowing you to maintain some upside potential if the underlying moves in your favor.

Convert to a More Neutral or Defined-Risk Strategy

Butterfly Spreads: A Butterfly Spread is designed to be neutral. If the stock doesn't move significantly, the options will decay, and the time decay works in your favor. A Butterfly Spread generally has a low delta and a higher theta (if you sell options near the money).

Iron Fly: Also known as Iron Butterfly, these are similar to Iron Condors but have the same strike price for the Short Call and Short Put legs. Iron Butterflies can help you create a neutral position with an attractive theta exposure, as the options you sell (the Short Call and Put) will have faster time decay.

Other Considerations for Adjusting Theta in a Portfolio:

Adjust Based on Time to Expiration: As expiration approaches, the theta of options increases (especially for at-the-money options). If you're managing a portfolio with multiple options, you may want to shift toward longer-dated options if you're concerned about time decay or shift to shorter-dated options if you want to profit from it.

Monitor Implied Volatility (IV): Theta and implied volatility are closely linked. If volatility increases, theta tends to decrease (especially for out-of-the-money options), meaning the effect of time decay slows down. Conversely, in low-volatility environments, theta tends to accelerate. You should monitor the volatility environment and adjust your positions accordingly.

Consider this example:

If your portfolio has high theta:

Strategy: You have several short calls and puts in your portfolio, resulting in a positive theta exposure. As expiration nears, your options benefit from time decay.

Adjustment: You balance this by buying some long options (negative theta) or rolling your short positions into further expiration dates (lower theta), thus reducing the portfolio's overall sensitivity to time decay.

If your portfolio has low theta:

Strategy: You have long Calls and Puts (negative theta), and your options lose value over time.

Adjustment: You start selling short-term options or implementing credit spreads to generate positive theta, which offsets the loss from the long positions.

Adjusting for high or low theta in an options portfolio involves strategically balancing positions that either benefit from time decay (selling options) or are adversely impacted by it (buying options). Whether you're trying to reduce the negative effect of theta or increase your portfolio's ability to generate profits from time decay, techniques like spreads, calendar rolls, and adjusting your option expiration cycles can help you manage theta exposure effectively.

BINARY EVENTS

Trading options around binary events—events where the outcome is either one of two possibilities (e.g., a company earnings report, a central bank decision, or a geopolitical event)—requires careful planning and risk management, as these events tend to cause significant, often unpredictable price moves. Although I typically avoid trading during binary events, there are strategies for trading binary events. Here's a breakdown of how to approach options trading around such events:

Understand the Binary Event

A binary event is generally a known (scheduled) communication of information that can reasonably be expected to influence a significant market move. Common binary events include:

• **Earnings reports**: A company announces its quarterly earnings, and the market reacts based on whether the results beat or miss expectations. Positive earnings reports don't always equate to an increase in stock price and vice versa.

• **Economic data releases**: Data like unemployment rates, GDP growth, or inflation reports can move markets.

- **Central bank decisions**: Interest rate changes or statements from the Federal Reserve, ECB, or other central banks can cause market shifts.

- **Geopolitical events**: Elections, referendums, or international conflicts can create uncertainty, increase volatility, and cause stock prices to move significantly.

You can locate dates and times of data releases by searching the internet for the U.S. economic calendar. Events that typically have some effect on the market have their time of release in BOLD. Those releases that almost always have a market effect are highlighted in red on most calendars.

Friday February 07 2025

Time		Country	Event
07:30 AM	🇺🇸	US	Non Farm Payrolls
07:30 AM	🇺🇸	US	Unemployment Rate
07:30 AM	🇺🇸	US	Average Hourly Earnings MoM
07:30 AM	🇺🇸	US	Average Hourly Earnings YoY
07:30 AM	🇺🇸	US	Participation Rate
07:30 AM	🇺🇸	US	Average Weekly Hours

Volatility Considerations

- **Implied Volatility (IV)**: Implied volatility tends to rise ahead of binary events due to the uncertainty surrounding the outcome. This increase can make options more expensive. If you're buying options, you want the IV to remain high after the event so the options retain value. If you're selling options, you generally benefit from higher IV because you can sell overpriced options.

• **Volatility Crush**: After the binary event passes and the uncertainty is resolved, IV often drops significantly, a phenomenon known as "volatility crush." This can drastically reduce the value of options, particularly out-of-the-money options.

Types of Strategies for Binary Events

Buying Options (Long Position)

If you expect a big move but are unsure of the direction, you might consider buying a straddle or strangle:

• **Straddle**: Buy a Call and a Put option at the same strike price with the same expiration date. This strategy profits if the underlying asset moves significantly in either direction (up or down).

• **Strangle**: Similar to a Straddle but with a lower-cost setup. You buy a Call and a Put with different strike prices.

The risk is that both options may expire worthless if the move isn't large enough.

Pros:

• Potential for large profits if the event causes a significant price move in either direction.

Cons:

• High premium cost due to elevated IV before the event. You need a large enough move to offset the initial cost.

• Risk of volatility crush afterward.

Run Before Earnings Trade:

A higher probability trade with less risk involves getting out of the trade before earnings. Because implied volatility rises just before earnings, the cost of options rises. This is good news for buying options. Look at the chart of a stock with earnings 2-3 weeks away. What has the stock typically done just before earnings? If you see a pattern of the stock rising six of the last eight quarters before earnings, you can look to put on a long position. As implied volatility increases close to earnings, you will want to close the position within a day or two before earnings.

Selling Options (Short Position)

If you expect little or no price movement after the event, selling options (a **Short Straddle** or **Short Strangle**) can be profitable. This strategy works well if you anticipate low volatility post-event or believe the market will settle into a range.

• **Short Straddle**: Sell a Call and a Put at the same strike price with the same expiration date. If the underlying asset stays near the strike price, both options expire worthless, allowing you to keep the premiums.

• **Short Strangle**: Sell a Call and a Put at different strikes. This strategy benefits from lower premiums but still requires the price to stay within a range to be profitable.

Pros:

• Profits from the decay of option premiums due to a decrease in IV after the event.

Cons:

• Unlimited risk if the price moves sharply in either direction, as your potential losses are unbounded.

• Requires careful management of risk and position size.

Iron Condor (Neutral Strategy)

An Iron Condor is a more complex strategy that involves selling an out-of-the-money Put and Call (like a Short Strangle) and buying further out-of-the-money Puts and Calls to limit risk. This strategy profits if the price stays within a specific range.

Pros:

• Defined risk and reward, making it suitable for traders who want to limit potential losses.

• Can work well when you expect low volatility around the binary event.

Cons:

• You need to be right about the underlying staying within a specific range, which may not be realistic during a binary event.

Calendar Spread

A Calendar Spread involves buying a longer-dated option and selling a shorter-dated option with the same strike price. This strategy profits from the passage of time and volatility crush after the binary event.

Pros:

- Can benefit from volatility decay after the event.

- Defined risk with a limited reward potential.

Cons:

- You need to be able to manage the spread effectively, especially if the event causes a substantial price move.

- Can be tricky to execute well if the event leads to a sharp price move, as you'll need to adjust the position.

Pre-Event Preparation

- **Research the Event**: Examine similar past events and their market reactions to assess the likelihood of large price swings.

- **Analyze IV**: Check the implied volatility of options leading up to the event. A significant increase in IV indicates a high demand for options as traders speculate on the outcome.

- **Set Expectations**: Have a clear understanding of what type of market reaction you expect (large or small, up or down).

- **Define Risk**: Binary events can create unpredictable movements, so define your risk tolerance before entering a trade.

Post-Event Considerations

- **Manage Positions**: After the event, manage your positions carefully. If you're holding options, you may want to exit quickly to avoid losing value due to volatility crush.

- **Consider Rolling**: If the market moves significantly, you can roll your position to a later expiration if you still expect volatility to continue.

- **Lock in Profits Early**: If you're in a profitable position, it might make sense to lock in profits, as the post-event environment can change rapidly.

Risk Management

- **Position Size**: Trading binary events can be risky, so consider smaller position sizes to limit exposure.

- **Stop Loss/Profit Targets**: Set predefined stop-loss and profit targets to exit the trade in a controlled manner.

- **Diversification**: Avoid putting all your capital into a single binary event. Diversify your trades across different assets or events.

Example:

Suppose a company, XYZ, is set to release earnings in 2 weeks. The options market is pricing in high volatility, and implied volatility has spiked. You expect a big move, but you don't know which direction.

You could:

- Buy a Straddle (XYZ 100 Call and 100 Put), profiting if the stock moves significantly in either direction.

- Alternatively, you might sell an Iron Condor if you believe the stock will stay within a specific range (e.g., 90 Put, 110 Call, and their respective long options at 85 and 115).

If the company's earnings report causes a significant move, the Straddle could make a profit. But if the stock stays flat, the Iron Condor would likely make a profit due to the decay in premiums.

In summary, trading options around binary events requires a mix of strategy, timing, and risk management. You must carefully assess the implied volatility, define your expectations for price movement, and manage your positions accordingly. Whether buying options to profit from a big move or selling options to capitalize on volatility crush, it's essential to understand the dynamics of the specific event you're trading around.

CONCLUSION AND KEY POINTS

Obtaining financial freedom does not take luck. It takes skill that can be learned. Financial freedom is a journey that offers peace of mind, reduced stress, and the ability to live life on one's own terms. This chapter is written as a summary and reference for you to use as you begin trading in your account.

Key aspects of financial freedom include:

1. **Passive Income**: Money earned without active work, such as traditional savings, 401k investments, investing in businesses that increase in value over time, or investing in real estate that appreciates over time.

2. **Debt Freedom**: Being free from high-interest debts and living within one's means.

3. **Emergency Savings**: A financial safety net for unexpected events.

4. **Active Income from Trading**: Earning money by leveraging a small amount of capital to gain a greater return by buying stocks, and buying & selling stock options.

5. **Lifestyle Flexibility**: The ability to choose how to spend your time without financial constraints.

After examining the traditional 401k approach, you discover it as an incomplete path to financial freedom. The 401k offers a chance to invest and grow funds for retirement, but it comes with limitations, such as limited investment choices and high fees. In market downturns, it's not uncommon to lose a significant portion of your savings, and the funds are locked until retirement age. While the 401k offers tax advantages, it doesn't provide the freedom and flexibility that financial independence requires.

Investing in real estate sounds great. However, it often requires large capital investments upfront and comes with great risk. Real estate is also not as liquid an asset as you might think. It could be very difficult to exit the investment if the market moves against you.

The key to financial freedom is living below your means, staying out of debt, and investing wisely. With the right investment strategies, it's possible to build significant wealth—far more than what a 401k alone can provide. There is a potential for trading, using vehicles like ROTH IRAs for tax-free growth, as a way to rapidly accelerate wealth accumulation. Trading is a strategy to achieve financial freedom, moving beyond the limitations of conventional investment methods and unlocking the potential for more lucrative opportunities.

Trading is the active process of buying and selling financial assets—such as stocks, options, bonds, commodities, currencies, and more—with the aim of making a profit from price fluctuations. Unlike passive investing, where assets are bought and held long-term (such as in a 401k), trading involves taking advantage of short to medium-term market movements.

- **Stocks** are ownership shares in companies, and they can be bought or sold on stock exchanges like the NYSE or NASDAQ. Investors profit by receiving dividends and benefiting from stock price appreciation. Stocks have a unique ticker symbol (e.g., AAPL for Apple, TSLA for Tesla).

- **Options** are contracts that allow traders to invest in stocks without paying the full price of the shares. They are bought in lots (usually 100 shares per lot). Options come with expiration dates and offer leverage—allowing traders to control a large amount of stock for a small upfront cost. While stocks and ETFs do not expire, options have an expiration date that varies based on the contract.

Key Types of Assets in Trading:

- **Stocks**: Direct ownership in a company.

- **ETFs (Exchange-Traded Funds)**: Funds that hold a variety of stocks, offering diversified exposure without buying individual stocks.

- **Options**: Contracts that give the right (but not the obligation) to buy or sell a stock at a specified price, by a specified date.

Active vs. Passive Investing:

- **Active Investing (Trading)**: Requires monitoring positions actively, but doesn't necessarily mean constant checking. Traders usually check once a day or every couple of weeks, depending on their strategy.

- **Passive Investing (Buy & Hold)**: Holding stocks or ETFs for the long term, without worrying about short-term market movements.

Leverage in Options: Options allow traders to control a large amount of stock with a small investment. Leverage amplifies returns, making options a powerful tool for traders with smaller accounts.

Risk in Trading:

- **Stocks**: If a stock price drops, an investor can lose money by selling at a lower price than the purchase price. Stocks can also stay in a consolidation phase, where their price moves up and down without significant gains, leaving investors "stuck" for an extended period, at times (think years).

- **Options**: While options offer the potential for huge gains due to leverage, they also carry risk, particularly if the stock does not move as expected by the expiration date. Options can be used in a variety of market conditions, allowing traders to profit from rising, falling, or stagnant prices. More importantly, the risk time horizon for options is much shorter. You could have a position in play for merely days, weeks, or a couple of months. Some plays could be a matter of a few hours. While this is not about day trading, you could have a trade pay off in a matter of minutes.

Types of Options:

- **Call Options**: Give the right to buy a stock at a specified price (strike price).

- **Put Options**: Give the right to sell a stock at a specified price.

Market Cycles: The stock market moves through periods of uptrends, consolidations (sideways movements), and downtrends. During consolidations (which make up about 50-60% of the time), prices may move within a range of resistance (top) and support (bottom), making it harder to profit in a buy-and-hold strategy. Options trading can allow profits in all market conditions, including when the market is consolidating.

Binary Events: Events like earnings reports, CEO changes, or Federal Reserve announcements can cause sharp price movements. Some traders often time their options trades around these events to capitalize on potential volatility, while some avoid them altogether to minimize their exposure to risk associated with not knowing how the market may react to this information.

In summary, trading involves active investing through instruments like stocks and options, offering the potential for higher returns with strategic use of leverage. However, it also comes with the risk of market volatility and the need for careful timing, especially around major events.

Market Trends:

- Bullish: Expecting the market or stock to rise.

- Bearish: Expecting the market or stock to fall.

- Neutral: Market trades within a range, often called consolidation.

Options Basics:

1. **Calls**: Give the right to buy the underlying stock at a specified strike price.

   o **Buyer**: Has the right to buy.

   o **Seller**: Obligated to sell if the buyer exercises the option.

2. **Puts**: Give the right to sell the underlying stock at a specified strike price.

   o **Buyer**: Has the right to sell.

   o **Seller**: Obligated to buy if the buyer exercises the option.

Strategies Based on Market Outlook:

1. Bullish:

   o Sell Puts (expecting the price to stay above the strike price).

   o Buy Calls (expecting the price to rise above the strike price).

2. Bearish:

   o Sell Calls (expecting the price to stay below the strike price).

   o Buy Puts (expecting the price to fall below the strike price).

Option Terminology:

1. **Strike Price**: The target price at which the option can be exercised.

2. **Premium**: The cost to buy an option (for the buyer) or the income from selling an option (for the seller).

3. **Bid/Ask**: The bid is the price you sell at, and the ask is the price you buy at.

Moneyness of Options:

- **ATM (At the Money)**: The strike price is near the stock price.

- **OTM (Out of the Money)**: The stock price has not reached the strike price.

- **ITM (In the Money)**: The stock price has passed the strike price.

Intrinsic vs. Extrinsic Value:

- **Intrinsic Value**: The value of the option if exercised today. Only applies to **ITM** options.

- Call Intrinsic Value = Stock Price - Strike Price.

- Put Intrinsic Value = Strike Price - Stock Price.

- **Extrinsic Value**: Also known as time value, it decays as the expiration date approaches. It's the portion of the premium above the intrinsic value.

Option Premium Components:

- **Intrinsic Value**: Only exists if the option is ITM.

- **Extrinsic Value**: Decays over time, reaching zero at expiration.

Factors Affecting Option Value:

1. **Underlying Stock Price**: Affects intrinsic value.

2. **Implied Volatility**: Affects extrinsic value.

3. **Time to Expiration**: Affects extrinsic value (the more time, the more expensive the option).

4. **Dividends**: This may influence option value.

5. **Interest Rates**: This can affect the value, especially for long-term options.

Buying vs. Selling Options:

- **Buy Call**: Want the stock to rise (intrinsic value increases as stock price rises).

- **Buy Put**: Want the stock to fall (intrinsic value increases as stock price falls).

- **Sell Call**: Want the stock to stay below the strike price (option value decreases as stock price stays OTM).

- **Sell Put**: Want the stock to stay above the strike price (option value decreases as stock price stays OTM).

Time Decay:

- The closer to expiration, the faster the extrinsic value decays. Options lose value over time, especially in the final month before expiration.

In summary, options trading allows investors to speculate on price movements or hedge positions. Buying options offers limited risk (the premium paid), but the potential for large returns if the stock moves favorably. Selling options carries a higher probability of a winning trade if the option stays OTM, but it comes with potentially unlimited risk. Time decay accelerates as expiration approaches, impacting the value of options, particularly for sellers.

Summary of Factors Affecting Option Pricing

1. Stock Price:

• Intrinsic Value: Affects only ITM (In the Money) options.

• For calls, a higher stock price increases intrinsic value, as the stock price moves further above the strike price.

• For puts, a lower stock price increases intrinsic value, as the stock price moves further below the strike price.

2. Implied Volatility (IV):

• IV estimates future volatility, reflecting how much the stock price could move within a given period (typically 12 months).

• Higher IV means higher options prices, since volatility signals more uncertainty and larger expected price moves.

• IV and Stock Price: IV is inversely correlated with stock price movements. When stock prices rise, IV generally falls, and vice versa.

- IV Rank (IVR): A measure of the current IV relative to its historical range. Higher IVR leads to higher premiums, making it better for selling options.

- VIX: An index that measures market volatility, with readings of:

  - <20: Bullish, relaxed market

  - 20-40: Neutral to anxious market

  - >40: Bearish, high anxiety

3. **Time to Expiration:**

- More time to expiration means higher premiums due to greater extrinsic value (time value).

- The closer the option gets to expiration, the faster the time decay (theta) accelerates.

4. **Dividends:**

- Generally, dividends cause minor fluctuations in stock price when paid, but don't significantly affect option pricing unless the dividend is unusually large.

5. Interest Rates:

- Rising interest rates generally have a slight positive impact on calls and a negative impact on puts, but this effect is typically minimal for short-term options.

The "Greeks" (Option Pricing Sensitivity Measures):

1. Delta (Δ):

☐ Measures how much the option price changes with a $1 change in the stock price.

☐ Calls have a positive delta (0 to 1); puts have a negative delta (0 to -1).

☐ Delta and Moneyness:

o A 50 delta is at-the-money (ATM).

o Delta >50 means the option is In the Money (ITM).

o Delta <50 means the option is Out of the Money (OTM).

- Delta as Equivalent Shares: A 70 delta call behaves like being long 70 shares of stock.

2. Theta (Θ):

- Measures time decay: how much an option's value decreases as time passes, assuming stock price and IV stay constant.

- Time Decay: Is more significant for OTM options and less for ITM options.

- Selling Options: Beneficial for sellers, as time decay works in their favor when the option expires worthless.

3. Gamma (γ):

- Measures the rate of change of delta. Important for understanding how delta will change as the stock price moves.

- A high gamma means delta changes more rapidly with small price movements, typically in ATM options.

4. Vega (V):

- Measures the sensitivity of the option price to changes in implied volatility (IV).

- Higher IV increases the price of both calls and puts (more expensive premiums).

5. Rho (ϱ):

- Measures the sensitivity of the option price to changes in interest rates. This impact is typically minor for short-term options.

Key Points:

- Stock Price directly impacts intrinsic value.

- Implied Volatility (IV) significantly impacts option pricing, with higher IV leading to higher premiums.

- Time to Expiration and Time Decay (Theta) are crucial in determining the extrinsic value and timing of option strategies.

- Greeks (Delta, Theta, Gamma, Vega, Rho) provide insights into how changes in stock price, time, IV, and interest rates impact option prices.

Where Do You Begin in Options Trading?

1. Choosing the Right Strike & Type of Option:

o Buying ITM (In-the-Money) options has a higher probability of profit than buying OTM (Out-of-the-Money).

o Selling OTM options has a higher probability of profit since they are likely to expire worthless.

o A general rule: Ensure extrinsic value does not exceed 33% of the total premium when buying options.

o Prefer monthly expirations for higher open interest (at least 100), ensuring liquidity for smoother entries/exits.

o Stock liquidity is crucial. Narrow bid/ask spreads lead to easier trades.

o Earnings dates can be unpredictable, so be cautious when trading options around them.

2. Timeframe for Options:

o The sweet spot for trading options is around 45 days to expiration (DTE). Consider closing trades around 21 DTE due to accelerating time decay.

3. **Fundamentals vs. Technical Analysis:**

o You don't need fundamental analysis for options; options prices already reflect fundamental data.

o Technical analysis helps determine market direction (bullish, bearish, or neutral). Simple tools like trendlines, support/resistance, moving averages, and chart patterns can guide your decisions.

4. **Trend Analysis with Technical Indicators:**

o Use trendlines to spot trends. A break of the trendline may indicate a trend reversal.

o Support acts as a floor, while resistance acts as a ceiling. Breaks in these levels can signal trend changes.

o Moving Averages (EMA and SMA) help smooth price action and show trends, such as using the 13 EMA and 34 EMA for short-term trends.

o Reversion to the Mean: Stocks often return to their average price (mean), visible through tools like Keltner Channels and MACD (Moving Average Convergence Divergence).

5. Key Technical Indicators:

o MACD: Indicates momentum, crossovers between the MACD line and signal line offer buy/sell signals.

o Slow Stochastic: Shows overbought (above 80) or oversold (below 20) conditions, helping with timing entries and exits.

o Divergence between price and indicators can signal potential reversals.

6. Trade Execution:

o When opening a trade, you'll either Buy to Open (BTO) or Sell to Open (STO).

o When closing a trade, you'll either Sell to Close (STC) or Buy to Close (BTC).

o If you sell options, you collect a premium, and if the option expires worthless, you keep the premium (similar to an insurance model).

7. Bullish or Bearish Trade:

o For a bullish outlook, buy calls or sell puts.

o For a bearish outlook, buy puts or sell calls.

o Naked positions (selling without any protection) carry unlimited risk.

8. Order Types:

• You can place a market order (quick but potentially at a worse price) or a limit order (better price control but slower fill).

• Time-in-Force options allow you to set how long an order stays active: DAY (until the end of the day) or GTC (Good 'til Canceled).

Overall, trading options requires understanding the risks and rewards tied to market conditions, technical indicators, and option pricing dynamics. With careful strategy and planning, you can successfully navigate the world of options trading.

Here's a summary of the **risk management** advice provided:

1. Trade Size and Risk Limits

- Avoid trading positions that are too large. Losing trades should not take months to recover.

- Follow a rule: do not risk more than 200% of the credit received. Example: If a trade earns $500 in credit, limit losses to $1,000.

- Risking small amounts makes it easier to recover from losses.

2. **Managing Buying Power (BPR)**

- **Allocate BPR Carefully**:

- Keep enough unused BPR to handle volatility spikes, which can increase requirements for undefined risk trades.

- **Use VIX Guidelines**: Allocate portfolio buying power based on VIX levels:

  o VIX 0–15: 25% allocation

  o VIX 15–20: 30% allocation

  o VIX 20–30: 35% allocation

  o VIX 30–40: 40% allocation

  o VIX 40+: 50% allocation

3. Diversification

- **Underlying Assets:**

o Don't put more than 25% of BPR in one asset, especially correlated ones.

o Diversify across different industries, asset classes (e.g., stocks vs. bonds), and volatility levels.

- **Correlation Awareness:**

o Avoid highly correlated stocks (e.g., peanut butter and jelly). Look for noncorrelated assets (e.g., banking vs. ice cream).

o Use futures like /ES (S&P 500), /NG (natural gas), or /GC (gold) for additional diversification.

- **Beta and Volatility:**

o Stocks with a beta above 1 move more than the S&P 500, offering opportunities but also higher risk.

- **Strategies:**

o Use a mix of defined risk (limited losses) and undefined risk (higher BPR exposure) strategies.

o Spread trades across different expiration dates to allow for market corrections.

4. Adjusting to Volatility

- In low-VIX environments:

o Use long positions to benefit from potential volatility spikes.

o Avoid over-leveraging, as low volatility increases the risk of sudden expansions.

- Large VIX spikes tend to contract quickly.

5. Technical Analysis Integration

- Use tools like MACD, stochastic oscillators, and Keltner channels to identify market cycles and better time trades.

Steps to Prepare for a Trade:

1. Check Your Buying Power:

o Assess your available funds and manage buying power responsibly, considering the Volatility Index (VIX) and your risk strategies.

2. Decide on the Underlying:

o Choose between stocks, ETFs, or futures based on liquidity, volatility, and other factors.

o Check for earnings dates if trading stocks to avoid unnecessary risks.

3. Choose an Expiration Date:

o Opt for options closest to 45 days to expiration (DTE) for better management and profit potential.

4. Define Risk Strategy:

o Decide between defined risk (e.g., credit spreads) and undefined risk strategies (e.g., naked options).

o Understand the trade-offs between risk, profit potential, and required buying power.

5. Make a Directional Assumption:

o Use market analysis to predict the movement (bullish, bearish, or neutral).

6. Decide Your Strikes:

o Determine the strike price based on your strategy, delta values, and desired probability of profit (POP).

Key Considerations:

• Liquidity: Focus on options with tight bid/ask spreads, good open interest, and multiple expiration choices.

• Volatility: Trade options with higher implied volatility (IV) for better premiums but manage risk accordingly.

• Strategies:

o Defined Risk: Limited loss but lower profits.

o Undefined Risk: Higher profit potential but requires more capital and involves higher risk.

Managing trades is essential for optimizing portfolio performance, mitigating risks, and aligning with financial objectives. This book emphasizes several critical aspects of trade management:

1. Risk Management:

o Adjusting the portfolio's risk profile through trades.

o Maintaining diversification and managing correlations between assets to reduce concentrated risks.

2. Adapting to Market Conditions:

o Rebalancing portfolios to align with changing economic and market conditions.

o Adjusting strategies for different market cycles, such as bull or bear markets.

3. Capitalizing on Opportunities:

o Identifying and exploiting market inefficiencies or undervalued assets.

o Reacting quickly to new information, such as earnings reports or economic data.

4. Achieving Financial Goals:

o Ensuring the portfolio aligns with objectives (e.g., growth, income generation).

o Adjusting asset allocation based on investment time horizons and liquidity needs.

5. Optimizing Tax Efficiency:

o Leveraging strategies like tax-loss harvesting and understanding tax laws (e.g., Section 1256) to minimize tax liabilities.

6. Performance Optimization:

o Maximizing returns by reallocating capital to outperforming assets or strategies.

o Rebalancing to maintain target asset allocations.

7. **Managing Volatility**:

o Reducing drawdowns during market turbulence using hedging or diversification.

o Smoothing returns to minimize short-term volatility.

8. **Practical Trade Review Steps**:

o Evaluate profitable trades (e.g., closing at 50% or 25% profit thresholds).

o Assess losing trades based on risk levels, potential for recovery, and possible rolling to extend expiration dates.

o Monitor trades nearing 21 days to expiration (DTE) to decide whether to close, hold, or roll positions.

By staying disciplined, following mechanical rules, and avoiding emotional decision-making, investors can achieve better trade outcomes. Managing trades effectively supports long-term sustainability, adapts to market shifts, and ensures alignment with overall financial goals.

Keep your portfolio intact by managing your portfolio. **Key points to managing your portfolio:**

1. Portfolio Diversification:

o The importance of spreading investments across various asset classes, industries, and geographies to reduce risk.

o Avoiding over-concentration in a single asset or sector.

2. Asset Allocation:

o Balancing your portfolio among stocks, bonds, cash, and other asset classes based on your investment goals, time horizon, and risk tolerance.

o Adjusting allocation as market conditions and personal circumstances change.

3. Risk Management:

o Identifying and managing different types of risks (market risk, credit risk, etc.).

o Employing tools like stop-loss orders or hedging strategies to minimize losses.

4. Performance Monitoring and Rebalancing:

o Regularly reviewing your portfolio to ensure alignment with your investment objectives.

o Rebalancing by selling overperforming assets and reinvesting in underperforming ones to maintain the desired asset mix.

5. Tax Efficiency:

o Strategies for minimizing taxes on investments, such as using tax-advantaged accounts or holding assets for longer periods to benefit from lower capital gains tax rates.

6. Adapting to Market Changes:

o Staying informed about market trends and macroeconomic factors that could affect your portfolio.

o Remaining flexible and making strategic adjustments when necessary.

7. Emotional Discipline:

o Avoiding impulsive decisions based on short-term market fluctuations or fear.

o Maintaining a long-term perspective and sticking to a well-defined investment plan.

You have been given actionable insights and practical advice for building and maintaining a strong, resilient investment portfolio, emphasizing the importance of strategy, discipline, and regular review. Other factors to consider are binary events.

Binary events, such as earnings reports, central bank decisions, or geopolitical occurrences, can lead to significant and often unpredictable price moves in the market.

Key Concepts:

1. Understanding Binary Events:

o Events with clear, defined outcomes like earnings reports, economic data releases, or geopolitical events.

o Market-moving events are highlighted in economic calendars with bold text or red indicators.

2. **Volatility Considerations**:

o Implied Volatility (IV): Increases before the event due to uncertainty, inflating option prices.

o Volatility Crush: A sharp drop in IV post-event can drastically reduce option values.

Strategies for Binary Events:

1. **Buying Options**:

o Straddles and Strangles: Useful if you expect significant price moves but are unsure of the direction. These involve buying calls and puts with the same or different strike prices.

o Pros: High profit potential for large moves.

o Cons: Expensive premiums and risk from volatility crush.

2. **Selling Options**:

o Short Straddles and Strangles: Profitable if price movements are minimal post-event.

o Pros: Gains from premium decay.

o Cons: High risk of unlimited losses if price moves significantly.

3. **Neutral Strategies**:

o Iron Condor: Combines selling out-of-the-money puts and calls while buying further out-of-the-money options to limit risk. Profits from limited price movement within a range.

o Calendar Spreads: Focuses on volatility decay and profits from selling shorter-dated options while holding longer-dated ones.

Preparation and Management:

• **Pre-Event**:

o Research past events and assess market reactions.

o Analyze IV and set expectations for price movements.

o Define your risk tolerance.

• **Post-Event**:

o Exit positions quickly to avoid losses from volatility crush.

o Consider rolling positions or locking in profits early.

Risk Management:

- Limit position sizes to reduce exposure.

- Use stop-loss and profit targets to control trades.

- Diversify across different events or assets.

Successful trading around binary events requires understanding market dynamics, managing risk, and choosing the right strategies. Balancing high volatility and potential profits with the risks of volatility crush is key to navigating these events effectively. One management strategy is to avoid these events altogether by not investing in certain underlyings that could be affected by upcoming binary events.

◆ ◆ ◆

This book offers a comprehensive framework for navigating the financial markets with confidence and precision. It emphasizes preparation, disciplined trade execution, risk management, portfolio optimization, and handling binary events effectively. These components, when applied cohesively, create a robust foundation for long-term success in trading and investing. The overarching theme is that a strategic, informed, and methodical approach is essential to achieving consistent results, whether you're a novice or an experienced trader.

Through detailed strategies and actionable insights, this bridges the gap between theory and practice, empowering you to make sound decisions in an often unpredictable market environment. Ultimately, this book advocates for continuous learning and adaptability as the cornerstones of a resilient trading mindset.

Success begins with thorough preparation, which includes understanding your strategy, aligning it with market conditions, and maintaining emotional discipline. Risk management involves protecting capital through calculated risk measures ensuring longevity in trading. Using stop-loss orders, diversifying, and defining risk-reward ratios are crucial. A consistent, rules-based approach to trade execution minimizes emotional interference and improves decision-making under pressure. Balancing diversification, allocation, and rebalancing strategies helps optimize performance while managing risk across assets. Special attention is required for events like earnings reports, mergers, or macroeconomic shifts. Planning trades around these events reduces uncertainty and leverages opportunities. Embrace Continuous

Improvement. Markets evolve, and staying competitive requires ongoing education, self-reflection, and refinement of strategies. Remember trading is a marathon, not a sprint. Maintaining a long-term perspective while managing short-term volatility is essential for sustainable success.

TRADING STRATEGY CHECKLIST

In conclusion, here is a checklist I use for my core strategy. I refer to this as the **Toups Core Trading Strategy**:

Check open positions:

- Look on the trade tab, curve view, analyze, at each position to determine if the price is moving in the right direction.

- If you feel the price will continue to move in the wrong direction and there is not much time for correction, look at rolling the trade or close the trade.

- Review the P/L Opn% on positions to determine if 50% or above. Close debit positions at 100%. If close to ½ way to DTE, close at 90-95%; Close Credit trade positions at 50%.

- Review DTE on positions. At 21 DTE, or the halfway mark on shorter time frames, close for profit or look to roll position for a credit.

Roll positions:

\- On a credit trade, see if you can roll out an OTM for a credit. If not, roll the untested side for a better breakeven, or roll out to allow time for play to work.

\- Always roll for a credit on credit trades.

Look to open new positions:

Do a daily checklist for the big picture and key equity sectors. This will give you an assumption of the market and sector direction. What does the trend look like for the market as a whole?

For Indices (SPX, NDX, IWM)

• When 8 EMA > 21 EMA we are in "buy mode", bullish trades are favored

• When 8 EMA < 21 EMA we are in "sell mode", can consider bearish trades

For individual stocks

• When 13 EMA > 34 EMA we are in "buy mode", bullish trades are favored

• When 13 EMA < 34 EMA we are in "sell mode" and can consider bearish trades

- Check buying power. Do you have buying power available (below 50% or below 70% if mainly debit trading)?

- Is the VIX => 20? If yes, look for credit trades. If not, look for debit trades.

- The idea is to buy high and sell low. If a stock is in an uptrend, you are looking for dips. If it is in a strong downtrend, you are looking for rips. Basically, pullbacks are where you can "buy the dips and sell the rips." Search watchlists for possible trades. Start by loading the saved scans in TOS to run "scans in all optionable"

- Use your favorites watchlist for earnings trades to check for possible trades

- Look for credit trades by searching 5 day change in IVx and look for green. Then sort by IVR. Look for High IVR (above 20-30), and IV (above 50%).

- Look for good liquidity (3+ stars).

- High open interest on the options you want to trade, over 10 per lot

- Does not have earnings from today until a few days before expiry. Earnings no closer than 14 days on a debit trade, unless you are doing the earnings trades.

- Closest to 30-65 DTE.

- Look for short positions <16 Δ or >85% OTM. Long positions 70 Δ.

- Extrinsic value of the options < 33% (1/3) of the total option premium.

- When selecting a strategy to use, look for ROC >=20%.

- Check that POP >50% on strategy. Review the analysis tab before sending. Minimum of 70% POP on credit trades, preferably 80%

- Enter a trade (long or short) when price is near the mean – when price is within +/- 1 ATR of the mean.

- Look for an entry signal. Enter a bullish trade after a candle has closed above the high of the low bar. Enter a bearish trade after a candle has closed below the low of the high bar.

- Trade bullish stocks in a bullish manner. Buy calls or sell puts near the mean on stocks trending up.

- Trade bearish stocks in a bearish manner. Buy puts or sell calls near the mean on stocks trending down.

- Exit either at mental stop loss, or point of validity.

o Credit trade is 150%-200% loss

o Debit trade is near 90% loss

o EMAs crossover to signal a reverse in trend

Glossary of Key Terms

1. Investment Basics

Financial Freedom

Refers to a state where a person has sufficient income, assets, or resources to cover their living expenses without relying on active work. It is the ultimate goal for achieving peace of mind and lifestyle flexibility.

Passive Income

Income generated without active involvement, such as earnings from investments, rental properties, royalties, or automated businesses.

401(k)

A retirement savings plan sponsored by an employer, allowing employees to invest a portion of their paycheck before taxes. Employers often match contributions to a certain extent.

Roth IRA

An individual retirement account is funded with after-tax dollars. Contributions grow tax-free, and qualified withdrawals in retirement are tax-free.

Stock Market

A marketplace where shares of publicly traded companies are bought and sold. It includes exchanges like the NYSE and Nasdaq.

Savings Account

A low-risk financial account where deposited money earns interest, typically offering lower returns than investment options like the stock market.

Index Funds

Mutual funds or ETFs designed to mimic the performance of a market index, such as the S&P 500. They offer diversification and passive investment opportunities.

2. Trading Concepts

Options

Contracts that grant the buyer the right (but not the obligation) to buy or sell an asset at a specific price (strike price) before the expiration date.

Call Option

A contract giving the buyer the right to purchase an asset at the strike price before expiration. Often used in bullish strategies.

Put Option

A contract granting the buyer the right to sell an asset at the strike price before expiration. Commonly used in bearish strategies.

Ticker Symbol

A unique series of letters assigned to a publicly traded company or ETF, such as AAPL (Apple) or SPY (S&P 500 ETF).

Bid Price

The highest price a buyer is willing to pay for a security.

Ask Price

The lowest price a seller is willing to accept for a security.

Options Chain

A listing of all available options for a specific stock or asset, organized by expiration date and strike price.

Leverage

The use of borrowed funds or financial instruments (like options) to increase potential returns.

Strike Price

The specified price at which an option contract can be exercised.

Expiration Date

The date on which an options contract becomes invalid.

Days to Expiration (DTE)

The number of days remaining until an options contract expires.

3. Market Trends & Analysis

Bullish

An expectation that the market or a particular stock will rise.

Bearish

An expectation that the market or a particular stock will fall.

Neutral/Consolidation

A market phase where prices trade within a range, showing neither upward nor downward momentum.

Candlestick Chart

A chart used in technical analysis that displays the opening, closing, high, and low prices of a stock within a specific timeframe.

Support and Resistance

Levels where a stock's price tends to stop falling (support) or rising (resistance). These levels help traders identify potential entry and exit points.

4. Options Metrics

Implied Volatility (IV)

A measure of the market's expectations for future price fluctuations of an asset. Higher IV suggests greater uncertainty.

Implied Volatility Rank (IVR)

A metric comparing the current implied volatility of a stock to its range over the past 52 weeks, expressed as a percentage.

Intrinsic Value

The portion of an option's price representing the profit if it were exercised immediately.

Extrinsic Value

The portion of an option's price attributed to time remaining until expiration and market volatility.

Moneyness

Refers to the relationship between the stock price and the strike price of an option:
• In the Money (ITM): Stock price has passed the strike price.
• Out of the Money (OTM): Stock price has not reached the strike price.
• At the Money (ATM): Stock price is near the strike price.

Delta

Measures how much an option's price is expected to change for every $1 change in the stock price. It also indicates the probability of expiring ITM.

Theta

Measures the rate of time decay in an option's price. Options lose value as they approach expiration.

Gamma

Measures the rate of change of delta in response to a $1 change in the stock price.

Vega

Measures the sensitivity of an option's price to changes in implied volatility.

Rho

Measures the sensitivity of an option's price to changes in interest rates.

5. Risk Management

Buying Power

The amount of capital available to make trades, factoring in margin requirements and account balances.

Diversification

The practice of spreading investments across various assets, sectors, or strategies to reduce risk.

Defined Risk

Strategies where the maximum potential loss is predetermined and limited.

Undefined Risk

Strategies where potential losses are not capped, often involving selling naked options.

Portfolio Allocation

The percentage of capital allocated to various trades or assets, adjusted based on market conditions and risk tolerance.

6. Strategies

Iron Condor

A neutral options strategy combining a call credit spread and a put credit spread, used to profit from low volatility.

Naked Options

Options sold without owning the underlying asset or offsetting positions. These carry high risk.

Strangles

A strategy involving the simultaneous sale or purchase of OTM calls and puts, profiting from minimal price movement.

Credit Spreads

Defined risk strategies where a more expensive option is sold and a cheaper option is bought to reduce risk and collect a premium.

Debit Spreads

Defined risk strategies involving the purchase of a more expensive option and the sale of a cheaper option to reduce cost.

This glossary covers the key concepts and terms to help you navigate financial markets and trading strategies effectively.

References

Kiyosaki, R. T. (1997). *Rich dad poor dad: What the rich teach their kids about money—that the poor and middle class do not!* Warner Books.

Ree, S. (2020). *The Tao of trading: How to build abundant wealth in any market condition.* Authority Publishing.

Rihan, Tony (2013). *How I Learned to Trade Like Tom Sosnoff and Tony Battista. Book One: Trade Mechanics.* Antonio Rihan.

Spina, Julia (2022). *The Unlucky Investor's Guide To Options Trading.* John Wiley & Sons, Inc.

Town, P. (2006). *Rule #1: The simple strategy for successful investing in only 15 minutes a week!* Crown Business.

Tastytrade, Inc. (n.d.). Tastylive. https://www.tastylive.com

www.ingramcontent.com/pod-product-compliance
Lightning Source LLC
Chambersburg PA
CBHW071019280326
41935CB00011B/1413